Making a

Discovering the Power of Neurodiversity on a Learning Safari

Katrin McElderry and Mark Stoddart

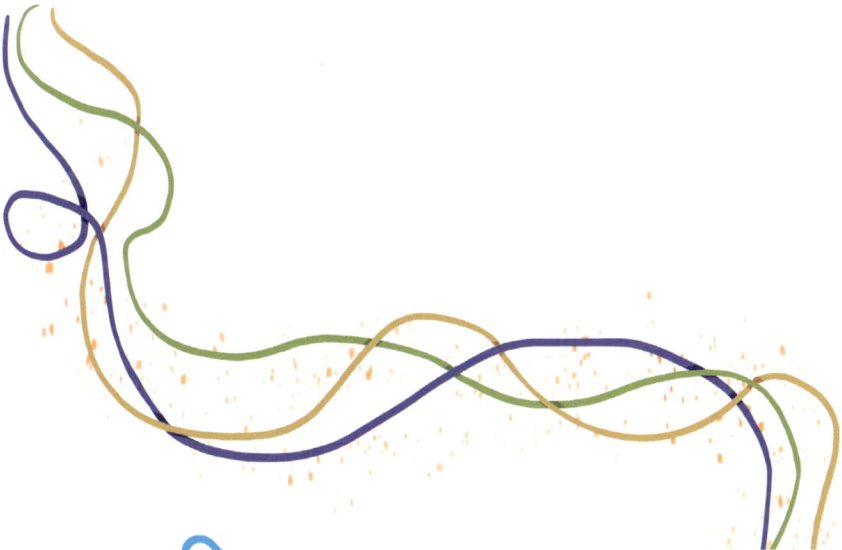

Brilliant
PUBLICATIONS

Dedication:

For my mother
KM

For Nel
MS

(and for all who celebrate neurodiversity and learning)

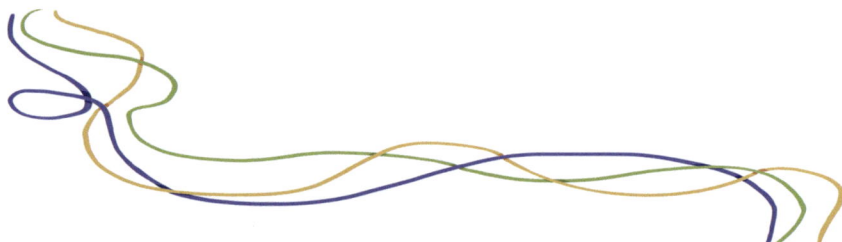

Published by Brilliant Publications Limited
Unit 10
Sparrow Hall Farm
Edlesborough
Dunstable
Bedfordshire
LU6 2ES, UK

Tel: +44 1525 222292
E-mail: info@brilliantpublications.co.uk
Website: www.brilliantpublications.co.uk

Brilliant Publications is a registered trademark.

Written by Katrin McElderry and Mark Stoddart

Illustrated by Rachel Cush and Rossie Stone

Cover illustration by Rachel Cush

Designed by Brilliant Publications Limited

© Brilliant Publications Limited 2023

ISBN: 978-1-78317-351-8

pdf ISBN: 978-1-78317-352-5

First printed in the UK in 2023.

The right of Katrin McElderry and Mark Stoddart to be identified as the authors of this work has been asserted by themselves in accordance with the Copyright, Designs and Patents Act 1988.

Dear Reader,

Years back, I was invited to listen to Mark Stoddart speak. Mark talked about his life and the role that neurodiversity and art play in it. He showed examples of his beautiful bronze sculptures and clever designs, and he also talked about his journey of learning and life. There were so many great messages and lessons behind his work that I was instantly inspired. After about ten minutes of listening to Mark share his story – especially about his struggles and triumphs with dyslexia – I knew that my students and colleagues would also benefit from hearing him speak. As soon as the talk was over, I shared with my family and friends – everyone I knew – more about Mark. Indeed, Mark is not only a talented artist, but an ambassador for dyslexia and neurodiversity. An educational champion, he kindly gives back to the world through his art and many projects.

I reached out to Mark to ask him if he would speak at my school and he did! For weeks after that talk, students and staff stopped me in the hallway of school to chat about Mark. They wrote me notes and drew pictures for me to pass on to Mark expressing their heartfelt gratitude and enthusiasm for the sculptor's story and work. I shared all of this with Mark and the fact that several students asked me if someone would please write a book about what his talks were all about. Well, Reader, the rest is history!

Katrin 'Kate' McElderry

Table of Contents

Prologue: StoddART 6

Chapters

1   Grimly Grammar 7
2   Mr Obliviay and the Morning Assembly 17
3   On the Spot 21
4   School Fails Mark 27
5   Learning in the Garden 31
6   Freshton College: A Learning Safari 35
7   Mrs Brill and the Morning Assembly 41
8   Mr Redwell: The Building Blocks of Reading 45
9   A Big Surprise 54
10   Art is the Key 58
11   The Key to Art 61
12   Bumps in the Road 65
13   An Animal Safari: Africa 70
14   At the Foundry: A Safari Ride with
     StoddART 74
15   Making a Mark 81
Epilogue: StoddART 87

Learning Resources

❐ Brain Basics: Brains are Unique! 90
   ❖   Basic Parts of the Brain 94
   ❖   The Cerebellum: Small but Mighty! 98
   ❖   The Amygdala: Learning is Emotional
       Stuff 100
   ❖   Thoughts on Working Memory 103

❒ Neurodiversity
  ❖   Dyslexia: What it Is and What it Isn't 107
  ❖   Dyscalculia: Not Maths Dyslexia 109
  ❖   Dysgraphia: More Than Just Handwriting ... 112
  ❖   Dyspraxia Takes Many Forms 114
  ❖   ADHD: Attention Deficit Hyperactivity
        Disorder 117
  ❖   We are ALL More Than One Thing 118

❒ Brain Plasticity and a Growth Mindset 120

Appendices

About the Authors 123
About the Illustrators 124
Learning Resource/Brain-based Information Editors.... 125
Wee Debrief: Discussion Questions and Reflection 126
Work Cited/ Notes 130
More Resources 141
Acknowledgements 143
Praise for Making a Mark! Discovering the Power
    of Neurodiversity on a Learning Safari 149

Prologue: StoddART

Good friends are gathered around me and nothing makes a table happier. A table? For real, a table feeling happy? I get it, how can a table be happy?! Sure, you can ask that to an ordinary table, but take a look at me. I am not your ordinary table!

No. Not at all. I'm a bronze hippo carefully crafted with a glass table top that is as crystal clear as water. I'm strong and enduring: standing the test of time. That's right, the timelessness of bronze, like the timelessness of friends who, today, are reunited; drinking their tea, eating their cake, laughing, chatting and remembering the ups and downs and how it all started …

Chapter 1

Grimly Grammar

Do you remember being just a wee child – a student eager to learn and ready to thrive? Well, if you had been Mark – a boy poised to learn and eager to strive – you'd never forget, because back in the day, there was once a principal, named Mr Obliviay.

Mind you, Grimly Grammar had some nice teachers, but the one who stood out the most, was not.

Mr Obliviay was the head teacher of Grimly Grammar. He had some mean and annoying habits. One was calling on students at random in class or all-school assemblies.

It didn't matter if the student was shy and not inclined to be put on the spot. No. In fact, Mr Obliviay quite **enjoyed** picking on students who **didn't** raise their hand and **didn't** want to volunteer. In fact, Mr Obliviay programmed the electric tassel dangling from his tattered mortar board to work something like a radar system. This helped him pick out the students to pick on!

Mr Obliviay also liked to emphasise the importance of **getting the right answers**, even though, in truth, he could be quite **wrong** about a number of things. In fact, he wasn't particularly aware of **himself**. Ha! Not even of the boil

perched at the end of his nose that flared up with his fiery temper.

Yet Mr Obliviay **was** aware of others' misgivings and had no qualms in pointing **them** out.

'Come on now Molly, recite the poem in full please. There's nothing to be nervous about. It's just the **whole school** watching. But let's **not make a mistake** this time, eh?'

Poor Molly. Shrinking in her seat, her eyes were fixated on the plaque above the door that stated **Grimly Grammar's motto** in English and Latin:

Learning is simple
Get the right answer

Mr Obliviay may have meant well. With a little more training and empathy, he could have become a kind and understanding educator. But sadly, Mr Obliviay dwelled in his own little world – a world with a narrow view of what smart was and what it wasn't. He was no mathematician in truth, but he made mental calculations, scanning the room, tallying up who he deemed worthy of his time and attention.

Indeed, his name was apt. Mr Obliviay was **oblivious** to students' needs, learning profiles, strengths and talents. When a student could spell Timbuktu or solve 5 plus 5 times **thirty-two** at **rapid** speed, he was only **too** happy to praise the pupil.

Public praise was all fine and well if you were a student who learned to read, write, and do maths easily and speedily. But not all students did at Grimly Grammar – just as not all students would anywhere in fact.

'Nicely done, Stewart. Now **YOU** will go far in life –
more than I can say for some students.'

Meanwhile, Mark, George and Breda overheard Mr
Obliviay's mumbles, grumbles and snorts, whilst sitting
together at a table.
They were trying
to do their work.

Privately, Mr Obliviay and colleagues, Mrs Thwart and Mr Gruel, conversed on the sidelines. They thought of the struggling students at Grimly Grammar as **less** than their idea of '**normal**' promising students, and sadly never got to know them fully. In fact, they missed these students' interests and talents altogether.

Take George, who found organisation a challenge. Sometimes it was hard to focus. He also struggled with his pencil grip and the spacing of words on paper. Mrs Thwart, his English teacher, said his writing looked like chicken scratch. But George had no trouble holding a brush and found that painting water colour, washed across a page, allowed him to feel free, imaginative and … relaxed. Something he rarely ever felt at Grimly Grammar.

And Breda, who found mental maths and multiplication tables maddeningly difficult, was more than the sum of her mathematical woes. Her fine renderings of cats, dogs, horses and anything from nature were **spectacular**. With extra time, she found that she could get the right answer when counting on her fingers and making pictures. Otherwise the numbers floated as an overwhelming muddle in her brain. Breda became frustrated when this happened. Yet Mr Gruel, her maths teacher, told her she should simply **know** her maths tables.

'Fingers and pictures are babyish, Breda!' he insisted.

Breda knew better than this. Counting on her fingers and drawing out pictures **did** help. And when Mr Gruel wasn't looking, she went right back to it.

Then there was Mark. Sometimes maths could stump him too. Yet, it was words that vexed him. Reading and spelling felt nearly impossible to decipher.

Words came as one daunting lump, and Mark really wasn't sure how to approach them. He too would become anxious, especially when Mrs Thwart would demand him to 'repeat and memorise' in her piercing pitch. Mrs Thwart would preach that reading was just a matter of learning one's ABCs and one must try harder! She demanded, therefore, that Mark repeat long and difficult words **over and over again** and always in one go. Worst of all, she would actually laugh as Mark stumbled.

'Again, Mark. **Discombobulated**. Say it. **Disss** …'

Mark wanted to shout,'**DIS**?! … **DIS**respect! You are not respecting me nor how I learn, Mrs Thwart!'

But of course Mark never said that aloud (and he really couldn't get the word 'discombobulated' to come out either).

It was quite frustrating having mean teachers when kids could sometimes be mean themselves. It made school such a misery for Mark, George and Breda, or anyone else who didn't '**get the right answer**'.

The most ironic and infuriating part was that Mark and his friends were **not** imbeciles, nor daft. They were not unteachable or anything of the sort. No. Far from it. In fact, they were bright – very bright. And artistic … and keen to succeed!

But … Mrs Thwart, Mr Gruel and Mr Obliviay could not see this. What they saw were students who they assumed were:

a) slow

b) lazy

c) stupid

or

d) maybe all of the above?

Chapter 2

Mr Obliviay and the Morning Assembly

Monday began, as Mondays always did at Grimly Grammar, with an all-school assembly. The weather was reported – usually a version of 'drizzle' – and announcements were made. It was also when little impromptu quizzes were snuck in and sprung upon the children by the head teacher, Mr Obliviay.

Mr Obliviay loved calling on students at random. He would tower over them at the ready with his questions. On one particular morning, he called on young Mark from Mrs Thwart's homeroom class. Ill-tempered, like Mr Obliviay,

Mrs Thwart was like a wart: callous. She nodded in approval.

Mr Obliviay's eyes scanned the rows of students. He spotted Mark. Quiet and compliant, Mark stood up nervously.

'Good morning Mark!'

Mark thought to himself, 'Um, more like, **bad** morning!'

Mr Obliviay was oblivious to Mark's reluctance and plowed ahead.

'Now, Mark, do tell us the answer to the question,' Mr Obliviay demanded. Mark answered reluctantly, fumbling with his uniform.

'I believe it is, 16, sir,' Mark replied.

Mrs Thwart and Mr Obliviay exchanged glances. They were flabbergasted in disbelief.

'Well done, Mark … amazing … ha!'

Mrs Thwart chimed in, 'I am beside myself. Who would have thought **MARK** of all people could actually get the right **MARK**?!'

George whispered to Breda, 'Another one of Mrs Thwart's super **bad** jokes.'

Seated next to each other, the two exchanged worried glances as the other kids at school squirmed and whispered mean words.

Meanwhile, you could almost read what Mrs Thwart and Mr Obliviay were thinking. It was if they had a weighing scale with George, Breda, and Mark (and sometimes Molly) on the one side – and the other kids on the other side. It felt like the teachers had decided that some pupils just didn't measure up.

Regardless, the fact was, Mark **did** hit the mark! He got the right answer and was momentarily elated.

'Yippee,' he thought. 'I got the right answer!' Yet it was only to feel – a split second later – the sting of the half compliments the teachers had given him.

'Why couldn't they leave it at, well done?' Mark wondered. He was crestfallen.

Just then, Mr Obliviay went over to have a quick conference with Mrs Thwart. He returned to the podium to deliver an impromptu announcement in front of the school.

'Mark here has surprised us all at Grimly Grammar at how he stood up in front of all of you and gave the **right answer**. We have thus decided to have another all-school assembly tomorrow to give him a second opportunity to get the **right answer**. If he can get the **right answer** again, then we will give everyone a half day off school in celebration.'

The pupils of Grimly all cheered with enthusiasm and Mr Gruel, the maths teacher was equally excited.

A half day off school on a Tuesday!? Imagine it! Unheard of!

Mark froze. He looked over to his friends for moral support. George and Breda gave him knowing looks, for they understood themselves how hard it could be to get the **right answer**.

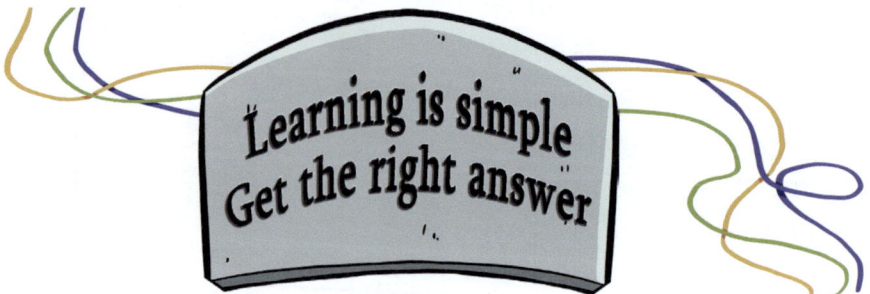

Learning is simple
Get the right answer

Chapter 3

On the Spot

Mark arrived at school the next day, hands sweaty and feeling anxious about the all-school assembly. Self-doubt overcame him, but Breda's and Mark's eyes met. George and Breda mouthed encouraging words from across the room.

'You've got this Mark! Go Mark!'

'You **can do it**, Mark!' They told him from afar.

'I can do it, if only I know the blooming answer!' Mark thought.

Mark was then called up on stage.

This time, Mr Gruel, the maths teacher, asked the question. Mr Gruel was rigid in posture (and unfortunately in his thinking too). He was exceptionally good-looking and young – so young it was almost as if he was trying to **compete** with the students. And guess who always won?

Mr Gruel pressed on, 'Mark, what is 13 times …' Mark was **paralysed** in fear – feeling the pulse of everyone around him in the large assembly hall. It felt like the room itself was alive and the walls were folding in on him.

'Think, think!' he told himself. He looked out onto the audience and felt the pressure building.

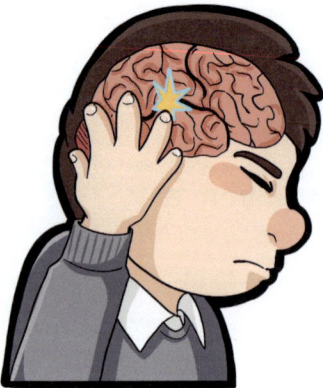

Grimly Grammar's staff and students were depending on him. They all wanted the day **off**! Mark couldn't even hear the last part of Mr Gruel's question. He really couldn't think. And if he couldn't think, how was he possibly able to **get the right answer**?

The audience was waiting. Their eyes were even more fixated upon Mark. At this point Mark's brain was taxed. He felt drowned in worry and sweat.

The staff and students fidgeted and murmured.
George and Breda were worried sick for their friend.
Mr Gruel tapped his clipboard, chiding him on, 'Mark, we're **w a i t - i n g** .'

Mr Obliviay, once again unaware that Mark did **not** want to be put on the spot, stepped in.

'Well, Mark, I'm afraid that is **not the right answer** and children, go on back to class as there will be no half day.'
The students groaned, and so did Mr Gruel, who was now feeling a bit resentful that he did not get the day off.
Mr Obliviay, with his boil inflamed and nostrils flared, called for order.

'Enough of that – go on back to your classes, assembly is over.'

Mark walked into maths class. He wished he could make himself disappear.

To add insult to the matter, he had to face Mr Gruel all over again.

'Mark,' Mr Gruel spoke. 'You will spend the rest of class over **here**,' he stated, pointing to a rickety old stool. Mark followed the teacher to the corner of the room. Mr Gruel continued.

'Now, as you sit here, you can be thinking about what the right answer really is **and** how you've let an entire school down with the sun shining outside and us all hoping for a day off!'

As the childish man said this, he ceremoniously put a dunce cap on Mark's head and pointed to the stool. Some kids giggled and Mr Gruel joined them. Laughing along with the students, Mr Gruel seemed particularly immature, like a big kid trying to play teacher.

The door to the classroom was ajar.

In the corridor, Principal Obliviay didn't realise that Mark could overhear him talking to Mrs Thwart.

'You know, I didn't think he could do it. Yesterday was just a lucky chance. He'll need a whole lot of luck, if he's ever to make a real **MARK** in life,' he chortled.

Mrs Thwart joined him in a giggle. Mark glanced at them and hung his head low as he sat in the corner adjacent to Mr Gruel, who began giving the maths lesson. Mr Gruel kept sniggering and muttering under his breath.

Mark thought to himself:

There is no one else like me …

This made Mark want to disappear because out of the corner of his eye, he noticed Mr Gruel was writing **DUNCE** on the board with an arrow pointing to the very spot where Mark himself was sitting. The fact was, this teacher had never been nice. But on that day, Mr Gruel was particularly **cruel**.

Chapter 4

School Fails Mark

The day of the dunce cap, the bullying, the ruthlessness of the teachers and mismatched teaching was the day it all became too much for Mark. Grimly Grammar wasn't a place of growth and learning, but instead stress and misery. Yet it would be true to say that not all schools were like this. Mark's parents knew this. They decided to look beyond their local village for other schools for their son.

Before they looked, Mark's father decided to have a word with Mr Obliviay and suggested he either take off his mortar board once-and-for-all or try to re-program the electric tassel.

Mark was completely unaware of this however and walked in on his parents' conversation at home. He overheard his parents talking in hushed tones. His mother was upset and burning papers in the fireplace.

Mark noted the papers had red **X**s all over them. One that was already burning in the fireplace said **Teachers' Comments**. Mark realised they were **his** papers from Grimly Grammar – and his mother was **burning** them!

Alarmed, he inquired, 'Mum, did I do something wrong? You're burning my papers from school!' His mother took a moment to answer.

'Mark, why do you think you did something wrong?'

Mark noticed that she had been crying. 'Mum, did I **fail** school this year?'

Mark's mum still did not answer. Instead she just crumpled more papers to put into the fireplace. Mark could feel a weight again – the weight of disappointment in the air. He felt utterly useless. He couldn't read or make his family proud it seemed. Just then, Mark's father decided to speak up and answered for his wife.

'Mark, the truth is **school failed you** and you will not be returning next term.'

Stunned, Mark was happily relieved, but also nervous and full of questions. He wondered and thought so many things all at once.

Ha! No more Mr Cruel-Gruel or Oblivious Obliviay or …

Then Mark wondered, 'Will I see George and Breda again? Will they still struggle? Where will my next school be?'

As Mark's head swirled with thoughts he watched the fire die down. The embers glowed and the school papers had turned to ash. The next morning Mark returned to the fireplace with a small shovel. His dog Kallie, a bull terrier, was by his side.

'Come on, Kallie, let's scoop up these ashes.'

Kallie barked – as if wondering or confused.

'They're my papers, Kallie. I didn't make the mark – I did poorly you see. I couldn't get the right answer and … I still can't read.'

Kallie barked again.

'It's okay Kallie, I'm taking it outside – the compost can use some ash anyway.'

Mark wandered off to his back garden with his dog and the ashes. He sat and reflected about the entire grim experience.

Chapter 5

Learning in the Garden

Days went by. The days turned to months and months turned to two full years of Mark not being in school! The ashes Mark and Kallie mixed into the compost pile had been spread on the garden as fresh soil many months before.

Mark was certainly missing school at **Grimly Grammar, but he DID NOT miss school AT ALL**. He did miss his old friends, George and Breda, however. He'd heard that they both had moved far away. Kallie, his faithful companion, kept Mark company, however, and they busied themselves in the garden behind the house. It was a good way to learn and a good distraction since his father had become ill.

Mark snipped off some fresh flowers.

'It's okay, Kallie, I am only cutting some of these for Mum to put on the table.'

Mark had been playing with his dog in the garden and also planting seeds into the soil, rain or shine. Verdant and expansive, the back garden allowed Mark's imagination to wander as he observed the beauty and growth around him. He marvelled at the process: how a seed, with the right conditions, could sprout, grow and flourish into such bounty and beauty.

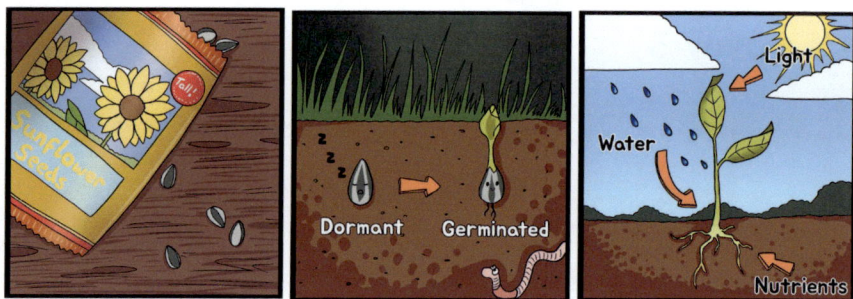

There were fruit trees, vegetables and flowers all in bloom and it was impossible not to marvel at it all!

Just then, Mark pulled up carrots in both hands, smiling.

'Kallie, **look** – they grew! Remember those seeds I planted!'

Kallie looked up as if listening.

'Kallie, don't you think plants and people have a lot in common?'

Kallie barked.

'Without the right conditions, the seeds simply never germinate. They remain dormant beneath the soil … . But **with** the right conditions, seeds can grow and thrive.'

Kallie barked in acknowledgement. She was a great listener.

'How simple and uncomplicated it all is – germination and growth. And yet how similar it is to being a kid in school! I am **so** glad not to be back at Grimly, Kallie. It's much better gardening and learning outside with you.'

Kallie still looked as if she was listening intently to Mark.

'But I can't imagine that I'll be able to spend my days in the garden like this forever. Let's hope my next school has gardeners for teachers!'

Kallie woofed and nuzzled.

'Recognise there is a seed of brilliance in everyone.'

Dr Peter Gamwell[1]

Several years later ...

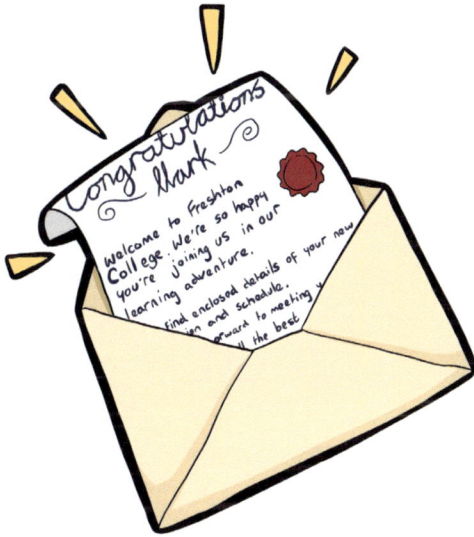
Congratulations Mark
Welcome to Freshton College. We're so happy you're joining us in our learning adventure. ... find enclosed details of your new ... and schedule. ... ward to meeting ... the best.

Chapter 6

Freshton College:
A Learning Safari

Grim Grimly Grammar now felt like a distant memory, (**thank goodness**)! Mark's life was taking on new chapters. His father had fully recovered and, with the help of his wife, had found Mark a new school.

The big day arrived! Mark's father stepped out the car near the entrance. His wife re-read the acceptance letter aloud.

> Dear Mark,
> Congratulations on joining our incoming class at Freshton College. We trust this will be a new and transformative experience for you as you go about the process of learning in ways that match your dyslexic thinking.

Mark was too distracted to take the letter in. Looking around the stately campus, it was as if his head and heart were elsewhere – and … well he **was** elsewhere. Mark was a long away from his village! He had never really been away from home – **and** he'd been learning and practically living in a garden with Kallie for several years now. Could he get used to being in school again? He had heard the classes were very small, yet there were **so** many students here and from **all** over. Although they all spoke English, most of them struggled with reading, writing, organisation and sometimes maths too.

Mark couldn't stop worrying. Had his parents made the right choice for him? It felt like a big leap of faith to leave home for boarding school.

Mark's mum continued reading the letter.

... and we trust that Freshton will be a place to develop passions and discover interests on your safari of learning.

Mark's father chuckled, 'I wonder what they mean by **safari**?! Sounds like it could be quite a wild ride, but then you've certainly already had that now, haven't you, Mark?' Mark nodded, but didn't join in the laugh. His mother piped up, 'Well, darling, not the **right kind** of wild ride,' but pointing to the campus added, 'this school really seems wonderful. Don't you think, Mark?'

Mark nodded, but still felt nervous and remained quiet. His parents moved past the wrought iron gates to talk to someone who greeted them in the entryway. Standing at the entrance, Mark stepped inside and took inventory. There was an assembly hall with student murals and art work on display. Teachers smiled and everyone seemed friendly. He noted a sign that said '**WELCOME!**' and a plaque above the entryway. The plaque said:

Learning is a process of growth and discovery

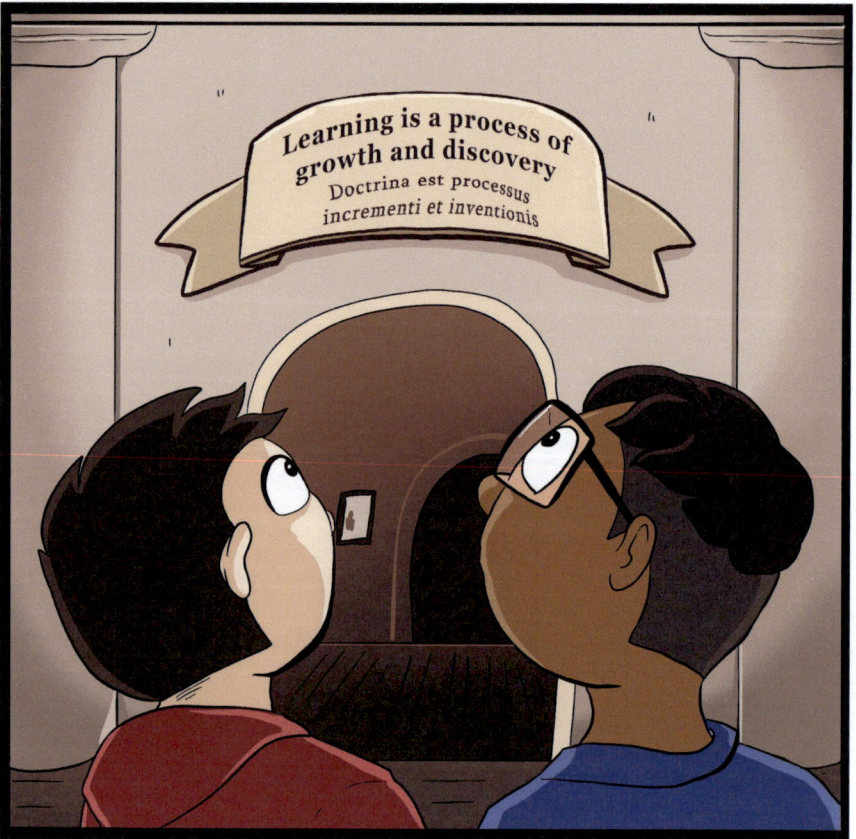

Just then a student nearby glanced up at it too.

'Hey mate, do you know what that says?'

'Ummm,' Mark hesitated. He felt put on the spot again until the stranger went on. Polite and confident, the boy added, 'You see, I'm here because I can't read … well, I can't read, yet! My parents put me in this school because there are methods to help people like me – and I guess you too, right? They say I'm actually smart – a big thinker – yet I struggle with some of the basics, like reading.' The boy shrugged, then put out his hand to shake.

'I'm Ian, by the way … and you?'

Mark, no longer felt put on the spot. Instead he thought to himself, '**he** struggles with reading too?! **I'm not the only one**??!! **FINALLY I AM NOT ALONE!!! There are other kids like ME!'**

I'm not the only one!

He struggles with reading too!

There are other kids like me!

Mark gathered his bearings and remembered his manners. He shook the student's hand.

'I'm Mark and I've just arrived.'

'Nice to meet you Mark! I arrived just yesterday.'

Mark returned to studying the plaque with Ian who was still chattering away.

'Yeah. I suppose I'm here for the same reason – I can't read … or I can't read **yet**. So, I'm not sure what the plaque says – not just the Latin words – but the English ones too. But I 'spose in time I will – or rather, we will.'

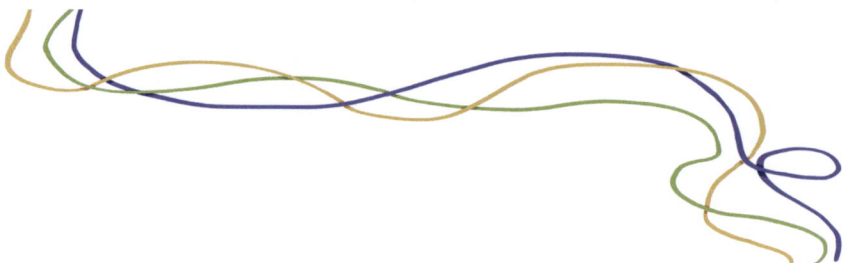

Chapter 7

Mrs Brill and the Morning Assembly

It was Mark's very first assembly at Freshton College. A woman stood on the stage. She seemed to glow with her warm eyes, big smile and brightly patterned outfit.

'Good morning students, I am Mrs Brill, head teacher. Welcome to Freshton College High School!

We are de**light**ed you are here! It's the first day and I know we can all feel quite jittery with nerves – hah! We've all had that one time or another – to be expected. Let's see, however, if you can channel that nervous energy into an excitement for learning: a learning **safari**!

The students sitting in the assembly hall listened with great interest, but wondered aloud, 'What!? For real? A learning safari?'

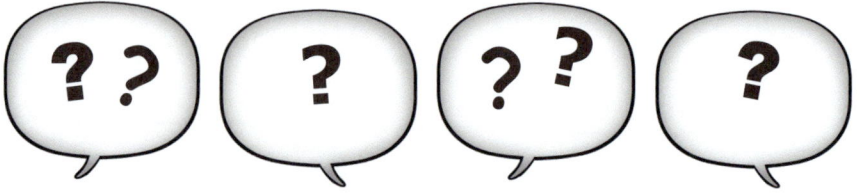

The woman was a seasoned teacher and read their minds. 'That's right – a learning safari! I wonder – can any of you think of how learning is like a safari?'

A few brave students raised their hands and Mrs Brill welcomed their ideas with great enthusiasm.

'… that's right, embarking on a safari ride takes an adventurous spirit! Anyone else?'

Another hand went up – and then a few others. Mrs Brill knew how to break the ice.

'… Sarah, that's another good point, safaris are most enjoyed with an open and flexible mind – agreed!'

'And I might add that every safari drive is unlike the other – every safari is unique …'

'… just as every one of you is unique!'

Ian was next. He raised his hand.

'One needs to be prepared – equipped – like school can help us do, I guess.'

Mrs Brill seemed to be radiating at this point.

'Ian, yes! And being well equipped will help prepare you for the unexpected twists and turns in the road ahead.'

Mark took in the moment. He was still a little nervous, but it was a good kind of nervous. He zoomed back into focus, listening to what Mrs Brill and other teachers had to say about the school. It really seemed like they understood that learning differently was just that – learning differently – and that learning differently was not necessarily a bad thing, that it could be, and often was, a really good thing. What a revelation this was to finally feel a weight lifted off! The weight of stigma and the weight of the dunce cap.

Mrs Brill concluded her speech, '… and we hope you'll discover that what was once seemingly impossible, is not!'

The new students at Freshton didn't entirely '**get**' how learning was like a safari. But they could see though that Mrs Brill seemed pretty brill (iant).

Chapter 8

Mr Redwell: The Building Blocks of Reading

Language class was about to begin. Mr Redwell launched right in and asked the students to introduce themselves.

'Hi everyone! Listening to you just now, it is clear that you can speak and hear. That's helpful because we're soon going to build on your ability to speak and hear well, **to read well**.'

Ian whispered, 'Guess that's why he's called Redwell – get it, well read, **READ-well**?'

Mark laughed.

'Students, we are very much focused on the process of things at this school. Stages and steps. Life itself is full of them. So I have a question for you. What is one of the first things you ever did as a baby?'

Ian whispered back to Mark, 'Now why is he talking about babies? We're in secondary school after all!'

Mark shrugged.

'They crawl and move around?' Sarah suggested.

'Uh, goo-goo, gah-gah-or-something.' Chris said with a laugh.

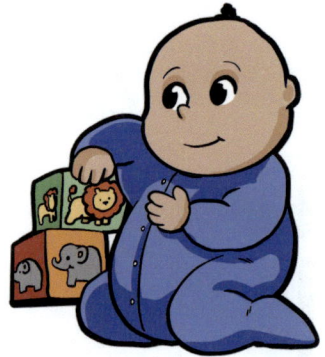

'YES, Chris … Goo-goo gah-gah-or-something is what we call **babble**! Baby babble. And the reason we bother talking about this is that **language** and **literacy**, include four parts: **listening**, **speaking**, **reading** and **writing**.'

Language + Literacy =
listening + speaking + reading + writing

L + L

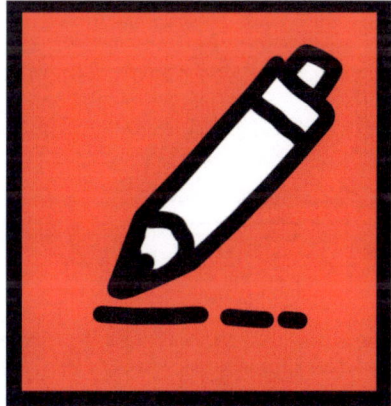

Mr Redwell ran over to his chart to make tick marks next to pictures.

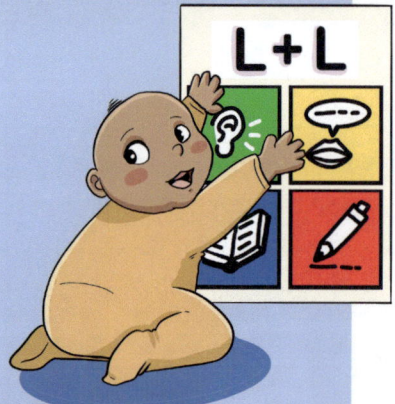

'You see – you have all mastered listening and speaking – that's two out of four skills,' he added, pointing back at the chart. 'So you're already halfway there!'

'Reading and writing are built on the very skills you began exercising as a baby: listening and speaking.'

Mr Redwell went on.

'Fun fact number 1: reading (and writing) are not natural in the way listening and speaking are. Your brains are wired to listen and speak. You've been doing that since you were babies. Yet reading and writing are different. They are human inventions.'

This caused the students to laugh a little.

'But sir, inventions are things like cars and computers.'

'That's true and reading and writing are too. And they are skills that have to be taught and learned.'

Lucia's hand flew up. 'With all due respect, Mr Redwell, everyone in this room has been listening and speaking well for over a decade, yet most of us can't read or write very well.'

'… can't read or write very well, **yet**,' Mr Redwell suggested with a wink.

This was the **complete opposite** of what Mrs Thwart used to say at Grimly Grammar. Mark recalled how Mrs Thwart insisted that reading was natural and as simple as ABC!

Mr Redwell continued, 'We can split words up into sounds and chunks to make reading easier. Then we can blend the sounds together to make words.' Mr Redwell's sound-based, speech-before-print method really helped the students to learn to read and write!

'Fun fact number 2,' the teacher continued. 'Learning how to read comes easily for some and for others, doesn't. But then we can say that about many things. Tying shoes, baking a cake, riding a bicycle, humming a tune – different things come more naturally to us, than others do.'

'But, with the right methods that match a person's thinking, we can all learn and improve on our biggest challenges in life – whatever they are.'

Mr Redwell passed out materials to each of the tables. 'It's all a process. And a journey.'

With a touch of teenage surliness, Chris piped up, 'Like a safari, Mr Redwell?!'

'Well … actually, **yes**!' And with that Mr Redwell flashed a smile and winked.

WoW!

Chapter 9

A Big Surprise

A few days later, Mark recognised a face coming out of the maths classroom. It was Breda – his old friend from Grimly Grammar! Breda was one of his oldest friends and what a big surprise it was to see a familiar face so far from home.

'Breda! Is that really YOU! **You're** here?!'

Huh?

'Mark! Oh my goodness!' Breda cried, 'you're about two heads taller now! How have you been?! And where have you been!? You never returned to Grimly!' she declared. 'Golly, gosh, Mark, I have a million and one questions for you!'

The old friends gave each other a warm hug.

'It's a long story, Breda. My parents took me out of Grimly. I learned on my own, then had a tutor for a short bit, and now … **here I am**!'

'Did you know that George and Molly are here too?'

Mark's head was practically spinning at this point. He was elated, 'So wait, I'm not the only one from Grimly Grammar?!'

I'm really NOT the only one!

'Nope. You're **not** the only one,' Breda confirmed.

'So … where to start, Breda? You seem well! Do you like it here?'

'I love it here,' Breda chirped. 'Everyone is kind and brings with them something unique. In my case, I am able to learn **my** way – and at **my** pace without Mr Cruel – I mean – **Gruel** hurrying me along and making me feel like my brain is complete rubbish. The maths teacher here, Dr Calcoolya, is totally different too – in fact she's **cool**!

'Wait, she is a doctor?' Mark asked.

'Well, yes, a certain type of doctor. She's our maths teacher and a scientist too. I have struggled understanding quantities in the past, but she's definitely taught me that we are all more than one thing, Mark.'

'Cool.'

'Yeah, but technically, Cal-**COOL**ya.' Breda replied with wink and continued, 'she actually **encourages** me to use my fingers to count, draw pictures, and take my time. I have improved so much that I nailed my multiplication tables.'

'Multiplication is tough for me too. It's why I'm in this class.'

'Mark, no worries. You'll get better in no time. I have been here for two years now and can you believe I am on to **algebra**?'

'Whoa! Algebra is **tough** – that's **great**!'

'I know it. I'm learning algebra using a scale and blocks.'

'It might look like I'm playing with toys – and heck – maybe I am, but Mark I'm really learning the way my brain works.'

'We're using blocks in reading – well, sort of – blocks representing units of sound. We break down the words into sounds, then build them up again and add on to them. Crazy as it seems, it's already making sense to me.'

'Hooray Mark! I'm not at all surprised … the teachers here are a little quirky, but at the end of the day, they know how to teach!'

'Yeah,' Mark said shaking his head, still in disbelief. 'I can't believe you and the others are here … and that I am learning like this. It's **so** different from Grimly.'

'Ha, no kidding Mark. Grimly was grim.'

Chapter 10

Art is the Key

As if saving the best for last, art class was scheduled at the end of the school day. Entering the studio, Mark noticed a portly, bearded man. It was the teacher, Mr O'Toole, who was unloading a kiln full of ceramic sculptures. Students were working independently at easels and tables as the teacher walked around giving feedback.

A beautiful painting caught Mark's eye – it was gigantic and mural-sized with swathes of colours blending, dripping, and mixing into each other. The brush strokes looked strangely familiar. Just then, the student returned to his work.

George! It was true what Breda had said, George was a student at Freshton now! When the two young students met, they patted each other on the back and dived into conversation.

'**Mark**! Breda said you were here! Whatssup! How are you!?'

Mark smiled and let out a sigh.

'I'm well and it's so good to see you, George! Everything is great here, but … well, to be perfectly honest, I'm a little overwhelmed. Things didn't end on a good note at Grimly … then I was at home … my father was ill, but now things are better.'

George listened compassionately while Mark continued, 'I guess you could say Freshton is a fresh new start for me. I am learning everything new. New, new, new! My sums, reading, writing; the dorm, the people, everything. It's like **BAM** – all at once.'

'Mark, it's brilliant seeing you too! Change can be hard, take it all step by step. Today's class might even help you. We're doing **Mindful Art**.'

'Never heard of it,' Mark chuckled. 'Sounds like something new, George!'

Four years later ...

Chapter 11

The Key to Art

It was nearing the end of the school year. Graduation day was fast approaching. Mark had no idea what he wanted to do after Freshton. Nevertheless, it was an exciting time. He and his classmates thrived from being a part of a community where people appreciated different thinkers.

Mr O'Toole's hair was pure white now. He was an older man, but none the less sharp than the first day Mark had met him four years earlier. The art teacher had a knack for spotting students' strengths and continued to encourage students like George to keep painting, Breda to keep drawing and Mark to work in 3-D.

'Mark, keep at it –
that wood is coming to
life you know.'

'Thanks, Mr O'Toole.
I like the idea of
having people look at
something from different
angles.'

'Mark, you're on to
something – **different
angles bring about
different perspectives**.
And that's just one of
the ways art makes the
world better.'

'Hmmm,' Mark thought aloud; but instead of it being
a question, he re-stated it slowly. '**Art makes the world
better – a better place**,' he added.

'Yes. Art is many things
and takes many forms. At
its essence it reminds us
that we're all human: born to
learn and create.'

'I like that idea
Mr O'Toole.'

The man nodded. 'Mark, you need to run with that creative energy of yours and you've only just a short bit of time left here at Freshton. I've decided to entrust you with the key to the studio. My hope is the space and the quiet will help further your artistic process.'

Mr O'Toole handed the key over to Mark.

Mark realised that holding the key to the art studio was a real honour. A sign of not only trust, but **belief** – belief in his potential. Mark was grateful for use of the space and Mr O'Toole's encouragement, for it was just dawning on him that the power of art was part of his own toolbox of skills, and a way for him to **make a mark**.

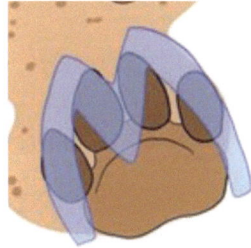

'Thank you Mr O'Toole – for everything.' Mark said, returning the key weeks later. Mr O'Toole nodded and smiled.

'Keep creating Mark, you're on to something.' Mark felt bittersweet – perhaps in part because it was awards ceremony and graduation day.

Proudly donning his cap and gown, Mark joined his classmates in the assembly hall. Mr O'Toole, Mr Redwell, Dr Calcoolya and other teachers joined Mrs Brill as she invited students on to the stage. Mark suddenly remembered being at Grimly – being called to the stage and later demoted to wearing a dunce cap. This school had built him up. What a difference Freshton had made in his life. He had come **so** far.

There was clapping in the big hall. Mark was next.

'Thank you for your contributions!' Mrs Brill said, handing Mark a special award and diploma. All of the graduating students were recognised for their talents, strengths and accomplishments. It made Mark so happy and grateful to be part of a place that made him, and every single one of the other students, feel truly part of something special. A community.

With his luggage packed up, Mark joined his parents in the car. They looked proud. Perhaps for the first time in his life, Mark felt proud.

'Mrs Brill was right,' Mark reflected to himself. 'Learning at Freshton was like a safari – wild, unexpected and brimming with memories.' But just as the car drove away Mark felt a bittersweet feeling again. He wondered, 'Now what?'

Chapter 12

Bumps in the Road

After high school, Mark tried many things, such as marketing and advertising. For a stint, he worked for his father's pharmaceutical company as well.

After a few years he was ready for a new adventure. Mark interviewed for a job with an insurance company. The interviewer saw immediately that Mark was able to anticipate problems before they happened and that when they did happen, he could solve them creatively. Mark's learning difficulties of the past had made him hard-working and resilient. He was kind and empathetic towards others. In short, he was perfect for the job! The supervisor offered Mark the job on the spot.

'Mark, you have all the qualities we are looking for and more. Sign here and then we'll go meet the head of the company.'

How exciting – to be offered the job – **on the spot**! The boss, Mr Barkley was called down to meet him.

'Good afternoon.'

'Good afternoon, Sir.'

'Pleased to meet you Mark. You're a fine young man we can tell, and our top candidate. Before we get on with things, I'd like you to read this document aloud.'

The document was terribly long and packed with tiny print.

'What is this?!' Mark thought. 'Am I in a time warp?'

'Why do I need to read this **entire** document aloud with everyone watching?!'

'I'll sit. You stand in front of us. Now read, Mark,' the man commanded. Mr Barkley's voice boomed and startled the office workers, who stopped and stared.

Mark proceeded and stumbled over words. He took a deep breath and started again, but Mr Barkley interrupted him and exploded.

'**What** kind of **reading** is **THAT**?'

'Sir, I'm sorry. I **CAN** read, but reading long passages – especially aloud can be a challenge because I have dyslexi-.'

'Dyslexi-**i**-tis?!' Mr Barkley shouted in an accusatory tone. It was as if Mark had offended the man. Mr Barclay was incensed. Mark took a deep breath and prepared to explain. He was certainly used to people misunderstanding and having to advocate for himself.

'Ah, not exactly sir. It's called dyslexia and …'

'Just stop it please – before we all catch your dyslexi-whatever you call it! Stop and be on your way, Mark!'

Mark wondered how dyslexia had become a disease in Mr Barkley's eyes. It was dumbfounding, but Mark stood up for himself.

'Mr Barkley, it's dyslexia – a learning profile, not a disease … besides, see here,' Mark said handing him the signed contract, 'I've actually already been offered the job …'

Huh?

'I beg to differ, Mark. You **failed MY** test and I am the **BOSS** after all. This job ends right here and right now. Now you can see your way **OUT**.'

Mark was stunned. He had been offered the job – had been told he was perfect – only then to be told to **get out**!?

Mark felt small, stupid, and useless. It was like Mr Obliviay had returned all over again.

On the train ride home, Mark spotted a billboard advertisement for London Zoo. The sign had giraffes, elephants and lions on it. It reminded him of what Mrs Brill had always said. Learning and life were often like a safari – and that breaking down and bumps in the road were all part of it.

Chapter 13

An Animal Safari: Africa

Mark had done many things by now – jobs and travels too. He was using his hands again, much as he did in Mr O'Toole's woodworking class. Mark was beginning to see that art could sometimes tell a story, express ideas and inspire – sometimes better than words could. After months of working very hard, he decided to go on an adventure and take a real animal safari with his old friends, Ian and Mzumbay.

Disembarking the plane, Mark inhaled deeply.

'Yup – that's it! It **smells** like Africa!' Mark announced with excitement.

'But wait – I thought you've never even been to Kenya before?' Ian queried.

'Nope – I haven't, but this is **exactly** what I **imagined** it would **look** and **smell** like! It's breath-taking, isn't it?!'

Ian breathed in and smiled at his old schoolmates. 'Tis … it's just fantastic!' He announced. And with that the friends went on to the next stop of their journey.

Mark instantly fell in love with Kenya (and all of Africa for that matter). He could hardly wait to get exploring. Being in Kenya (and later, his other travels) reminded him of learning in his garden all those years back. Kallie wasn't by his side, but there were so many other animals to take in. Birds in flight. Reptiles in river banks. Large mammals grazing in the savannah … how lucky Mark felt to get to see them all on a real safari ride!

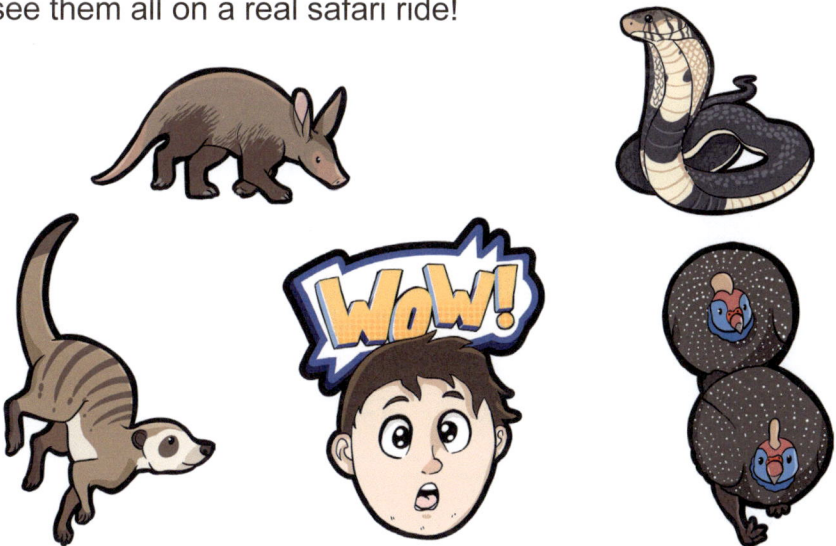

The safari driver took Mzumbay, Ian and Mark out into the bush. There were gazelles, giraffes and elephants in the savannah. Then they pulled up to a watering hole, which is where Mark spotted it – **a hippo**!

Looking awkward on land, the hippo was surprisingly graceful in the water. Mark suddenly realised, '**I AM JUST LIKE THIS HIPPO** – awkward in one place – at ease and successful in another!' He had a flashback to his own learning and thought to himself, 'the right environment – habitat for the hippo and school for a student – can make **ALL** the difference!'

It's true what Mrs Brill used to say, **expect the unexpected in life**, because the view was spectacular. The water was as crystal clear as glass and the sun was highlighting the hippo's head. The wild beauty of it all … Mark was completely inspired!

He pulled out his camera and while looking through the lens, Mark suddenly had an idea. A brilliant idea – a **dyslexic thinking** kind of idea! He visualised the design of a new kind of art – StoddART – a bronze hippo sculpture 'peering' out of a glass table top. Mark was loving his safari, but couldn't wait to get to his studio to make **StoddART** come to life!

Chapter 14

At the Foundry: A Safari Ride with StoddART

Back at the Foundry, Mark had a workshop. The building, which looked like it grew out of bedrock, was shared by many other sculptors and welders. Just home from his trip, Mark got busy. Laying out his photographs, he remembered his vision. Step by step, much in the way he was taught at Freshton, he worked steadily.

First there were the sketches, then the moulds to make, then the wax, the reveal, and eventually the patina to add. It was arduous and messy, with much trial and error along the way.

Back at the foundry...

Step 1– Making the sculpture

Clay

Step 2– Making a mould

Pink silicone

Step 3– Pouring the bronze

Molten bronze

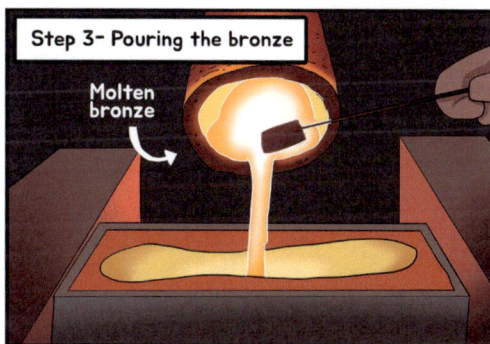

But eventually Mark managed to create a sculpture that blended form, function and great beauty – for the hippo seemed to be peering out onto a watery glass table top. In fact, **StoddART** evolved into a series of hippos, lions, tigers, elephants, rhinos and other animals with table tops too. These sculptural furniture pieces literally launched Mark's career!

After a lot of polishing and refining...

Stoddart is finished!

75

Indeed, Mark's work sold immediately and began being featured in magazines and newspaper articles. His work attracted much attention and even caught the eye of the British Royal Family at the annual Chelsea Flower Show in London.

Before he knew it, Mark could hardly keep track of the number of requests he had for sculptures and furniture – including pieces he had already made, as well as bespoke ones. In fact, families would ask Mark to make sculptures of animals they had seen on their own safaris.

Regardless, there always seemed to be a story behind Mark's projects and clients and some of those stories were touching.

Mr Stoddart, my father has terminal cancer and only has a few months left to live. We know a hippo table would cheer him up.

Mark hurried to finish that project, personally delivering and assembling the table right in front of the man's bed. The hippo table really did cheer the father up.

There were all sorts of other requests too.

Hello, Mr Stoddart, we have heard about StoddART – your incredible bronze work – and were wondering if you could create a sculpture of our pet.

Mark enjoyed creating sculptures inspired by people's love of animals and nature. He also loved making special pieces that celebrated history and technology. Whatever his subject, Mark wanted his sculptures to be functional and experiential – something you could touch and experience the 3-D nature of. When asked to make a sculpture of a model T Ford for display in a square in Fort William in Scotland, Mark decided to make it life-size and asked for it to be placed outside for the public to not only view, but climb into and even pretend to drive.

Mark's sculptures often required research, planning and working closely with clients. This was the case with former US Astronaut, Buzz Aldrin. Mark was over the moon to be asked to make a sculpture about the first moon landing. He visited NASA, met with Mr Aldrin and got busy!

Mark knew he wanted to make a model of the Apollo Lunar Module itself, but how would he represent it on the moon, he wondered? Mark studied his mock-up drawings from different angles. A-ha! He had it! He would make the glass table top the moon and etch in those famous words, 'One giant step …' and 'Magnificent desolation' right on to the glass surface.

Mark ended up making three versions of the Apollo table: one for Mr Aldrin, one for the Smithsonian Museum in Washington DC and one to be housed in the Scottish Parliament in Edinburgh.

Mark's pieces became prized collectibles throughout the world and connected him to many interesting people, some of whom have been important world leaders.

'Mr Stoddart, hello yes, this is Desmond – Desmond Tutu … . My friend Nelson – Nelson Mandela – and I were wondering if you might consider collaborating with us on a fundraiser here in South Africa to benefit children … hello? Mr Stoddart are you still there?'

Mark could hear loud and clear, but was so gobsmacked, he could barely speak.

Mark thought to himself, Archbishop Desmond Tutu?! President Nelson Mandela of South Africa? Whoa!!!

He quickly gathered himself.

'Hello … yes, still here … can hear you perfectly, Archbishop Tutu. **YES**! I would be honoured to work with you both and I love the fact that this project will benefit children.'

Mark became so busy making sculptural tables that now he needed some help. In time, he created a small team to assist him in some of the many organisational details involved with commissions and the design of new projects.

This also helped Mark find the time to use his art to help causes dear to him like protecting wildlife refuges, advocating for dyslexia awareness, and promoting art-based education in schools around the world.

Many decades later ...

Chapter 15

Making a Mark

> 'It is what difference we have made in
> the lives of others that will determine the
> significance of the life we lead.'
>
> **Nelson Mandela[4]**

It had been **decades** since Mark and his Freshton friends had seen one another. Yet the Freshton experience was never far from his mind. Its impact was immeasurable. The experience was simply **part of him**. Moreover, the experience had come full circle as Mark was becoming more involved in schools as an ambassador for dyslexia and neurodiversity.

When not sculpting, he was speaking, volunteering and overseeing details to create neurodiverse-friendly schools in places like Bali and Kenya that infuse best teaching practices and creativity.

As for connecting with friends, Zoom meetings were well and fine, but there was no substitute for the reunion Mark held at Lady Bank in beautiful Ayrshire, Scotland.

Mark greeted his old friends one by one and welcomed them into his home. The kettle was put on for tea and old memorabilia placed on Mark's first hippo table, **StoddART**.

'Welcome to Lady Bank,' Mark said warmly. 'Finally, we are all in one place again!' Indeed, it was not every day that friends from all other parts of the UK could convene, let alone those from Ireland, India, Bali, Singapore, Kenya, Australia, Belize, and the US too!

Mzumbay plopped himself at the table and called over to the others.

'Hey everyone, Mark's got his old yearbook out.'

'And I brought pictures!' Ian announced, spreading an array of old photos on the table for all to see.

Breda and Molly hovered over the old pictures. 'Oh my gosh – look how young we all looked!'

They all took turns sorting through the photos and flipping pages of the yearbook, commenting along the way. Indeed, it had been many years since school and they had all changed!

'Wayan, that's **YOU** performing in your costume! ... Ian, do you remember that concert ... and look here ... Mzumbay's collage from the senior show ... .

The friends sipped their tea and recollected on the past. They flipped to the faculty pages of the yearbook. There was a photo of Mr Redwell and his fellow faculty members.

'Oh my goodness, remember how Mr Redwell would go on about baby babble or something!' They all laughed. Chris was in stitches, 'Yeah … goo-goo, ga-ga or something? Yeah, he really ran with that!'

'How about when he made us **act out** punctuation to **get a feeling** for its usage?' Mark added.

George slapped his knee remembering … 'Yes! I remember. I felt silly, but honestly I finally got it. For commas he'd have us sit for a sec to feel the pause and then for a full stop-period, we'd have to stomp and put up our hand like a stop sign.'

'And don't forget the exclamation **MARK** that he'd literally have me **jumping** out of my seat for!' Mark chuckled as he jumped up out of his seat again, hearing the kettle whistling. He made a fresh pot of tea while the friends continued chatting.

They shared where their own safaris in life had taken them since Freshton days. Whatever they did and wherever they were in the world, they had all found their own unique path in life.

Take Breda, who had become a scientific illustrator. And Mzumbay who had become a doctor. There was Ian who was a school teacher and Molly who was a poet. Chris was an actor and Wayan a dancer. Lucia ran a business and George had become a therapist and painter. Regardless of whether they were artists for a living or not, studying the old yearbook reminded them that creativity and art had been an important part of their neurodiverse learning safaris.

'Isn't it amazing,' Breda reflected, 'how so many of us have creativity and art in our lives?'

'It really is—and to think that some of us went …

from grim …

… to a fresh start – to a life filled with learning … and **ART**.'

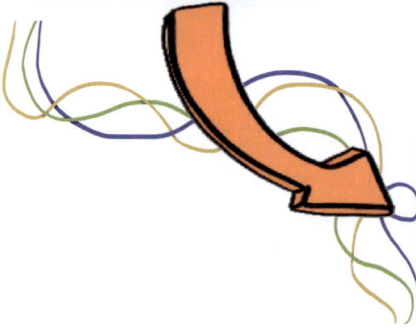

With that George patted the hippo table. 'And in your case Mark, it's been **StoddART**!'

The end …

Epilogue: StoddART

Well, it's not really the end, because Mark is still learning and growing and making his own mark in life through the power of art and neurodiversity. Like his friends, all living out their best selves, he knows that a learning safari never ends!

Afterword: Bronzes and Brains

It's important to note though that Mark's beautiful bronze sculptures first stem, not from metal alloys, but his **brain**!

Just as your ideas come from your brain, so do his. Mark's ability to notice patterns, visualise and interpret what he sees into a 3-D creation, reflect what some studies have shown about dyslexia. Some MRI studies have shown that some people with dyslexia have a well developed visual-spatial awareness.[5]

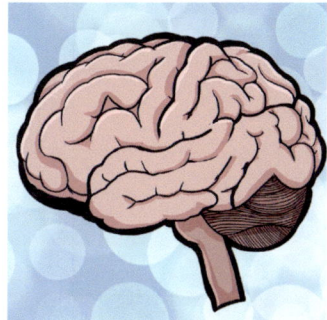

Additionally, brain scans have indicated that some people with dyslexia and other forms of neurodiversity may also have a heightened sensitivity to emotions, often translated as empathy for others: humans, animals and often the planet at large.[6]

Historians and other experts have also noted that people with learning profiles, much like those of the characters in this story, are highly creative problem-solvers and important contributors to society whatever their profession.[7]

But whoa … hang on there … let's not charge ahead of ourselves!

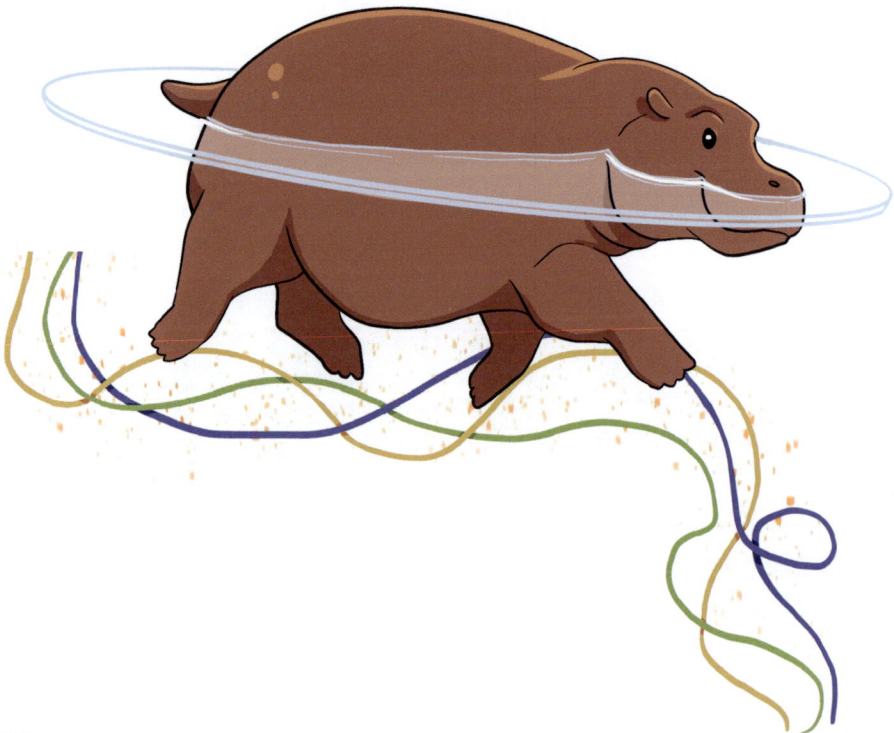

Learning Resources

First things first – a quick pause to explain about the pages ahead. The following section of this book is a learning resource. It is designed to teach a little bit about the brain and also shed some light on some common learning differences like **dyslexia**, **dyscalculia**, **dysgraphia**, and **dyspraxia**. Narrated by the Freshton students themselves, this is a chance to go on a little learning safari of your own!

Brain Basics: Brains are Unique!

Remembering What Mrs Brill Taught

It is worth stopping in our tracks to reflect upon this simple, but profound fact: **Every single person's brain is unique**.[8] One of a kind. Like no one else's on the planet!

Another stunning notion is this: **every** single thing you are able to do stems from your **own** brain power![9] Breathing, chewing, swallowing, sleeping, speaking, hearing, talking, walking, running, dancing, painting, creating …

It is all **BRAIN POWER**.

The brain is amazingly powerful! In fact, brain scientist, Dr Nirbhay Yadav shares some impressive facts. 'The brain consumes about 20% of the body's total energy but only accounts for 2% of its mass. That is 10 times higher than its proportion!'[7] Wow!

Some people liken the brain to a computer or the CEO of the human body. It both stores and processes the information it takes in. Neuroscientist, Dr Fumiko Hoeft calls the brain 'the conductor' of the body because it is an organ in charge of other organs that ultimately work synchronously.[10] That means that these parts work together.

This pinkish-gray, 3 lb (1.6 kg) organ is the very source of what makes up basic humanity.[11] The human brain is the root of thinking and intelligence. It is the interpreter of the senses you pick up in the world around you.

The brain is the initiator of bodily movements, and the controller of emotions and behaviours. It's so key to success and well being, that it is fair to say that learning about the brain empowers ourselves and others!

The brain really is a power house jam-packed with a complex network of brain cells called neurons ('nur-ons'). Your brain has about 100 billion neurons![12]

Neuron

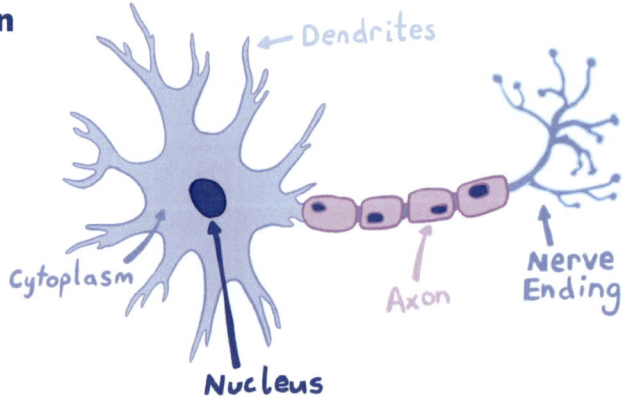

Neurons are electrically-charged, excitable cells that connect and communicate with other neurons at junctions to form what is called a **synapse** ('sie-naps' or 'si-naps' depending where you live). Messages are sent between neurons across a synapse using a sort of chemical or electrical bridge.[13]

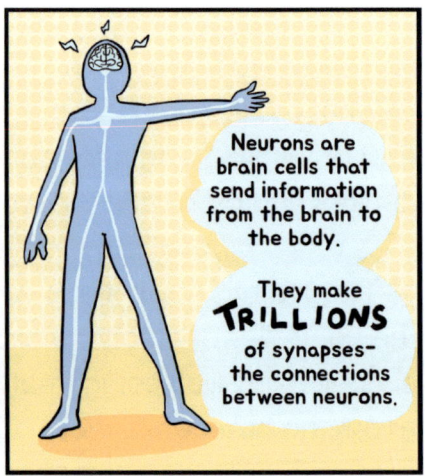

A synapse in action!

Neuron sending signal

Neuron receiving signal

Neurotransmitter

Receptor

Zooming in we can see the neurotransmitter moving between neurons

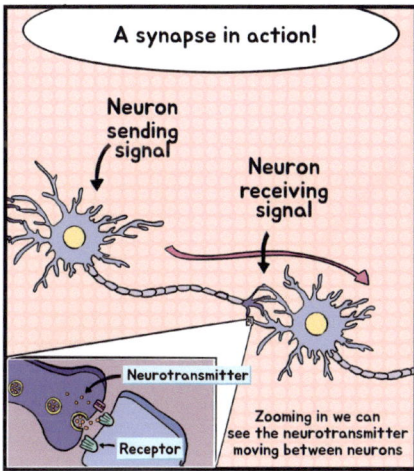

Different types of synaptic reactions happen over different time scales. Some processes take hours and they underpin learning and memory, while other processes happens within milliseconds.[14]

Some experts talk about learning in terms of strong or weak connections in the brain. For example, if a certain skill – like solving a mathematical equation – is a slow and difficult process, then learning new strategies with repetition and practice can help strengthen synaptic connections.[15] The connections made in the brain ultimately support all of our thoughts, behaviours, actions and feelings through the different parts that are responsible for different jobs.[16]

Fun Fact!

Neuroscientists often talk about neurons 'firing together to wire together!' [17]

Basic Parts of the Brain

by Chris

Recent research has shown that the brain is flexible, adaptable and **complex**! There is a lot to know about it and we won't be covering it all on this safari! The highlights here might give you a bit of an overview, however. What is probably most interesting to note about brain architecture is that it keeps building and changing through learning and experience![18]

Chris

Remember how Mark and Mr O'Toole were talking about different angles giving different perspectives?

That's true! To better understand how your brain looks and works, check out these different angles of the human brain.

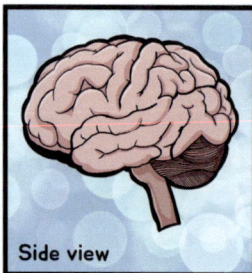

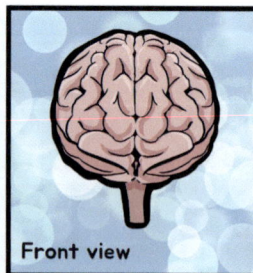

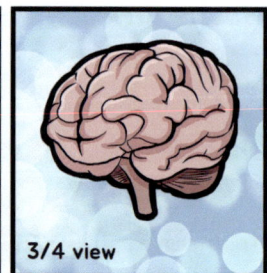

Side view | Front view | 3/4 view

The brain is divided into **two hemispheres** ('heh-mi-sfeers') that are connected.

Seated right upfront is the **frontal lobe**, which is in charge of executive functions, like scheduling to plan ahead, solving a mathematical equation, reasoning out an argument, coming up with ideas for a new story, as well as regulating or controlling emotions.[19]

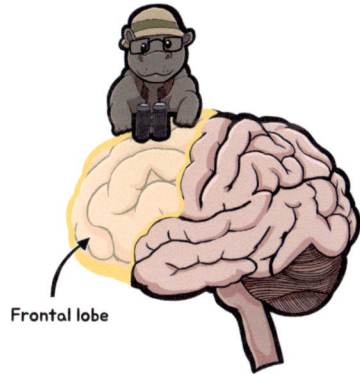

Frontal lobe

Right behind this region is the **motor cortex.**

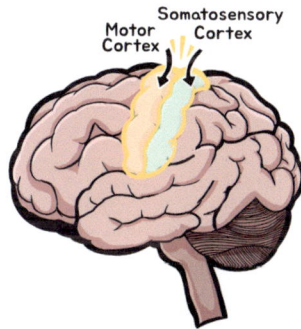

Somatosensory Cortex
Motor Cortex

This part of the brain is dedicated to **intentional** movement. This region helps with planning and the execution of voluntary movements like kicking a ball into a goal post or gripping a paint brush in a certain way to achieve the stroke desired.[20]

Just behind the motor cortex area, is a part of the brain called the **somatosensory** ('sow-ma-tow-sen-sr-ee') cortex. This region receives information about taste, touch, temperature and movement from the rest of the body.[21]

Move your way further back and you have the **parietal** ('pr-ai-uh-tl') **lobes**. This area is responsible for integrating information like vision and sound. It helps orient oneself in space. Dr Calcoolya also taught us that the parietal lobes are important for number sense and are related to space and in reading by integrating visual and auditory information.[22]

Moving towards the rear part of the upper brain, we reach the **occipital** ('ox-i-pi-tul') **lobes**. This is a region of the brain in charge of visual functions. The occipital lobes process images received from the eyes.[23]

Now approaching the last part of the upper brain, we reach the **temporal lobes**. They are situated right around the temples of a person's head – hence the name. The **temporal lobes** work together to process hearing and speech-related information. In fact, the underside of each temporal lobe retrieves and formulates memories. Scientists believe that parts of the temporal lobe also integrate memories and senses relating to taste, touch, sound and sight.[24]

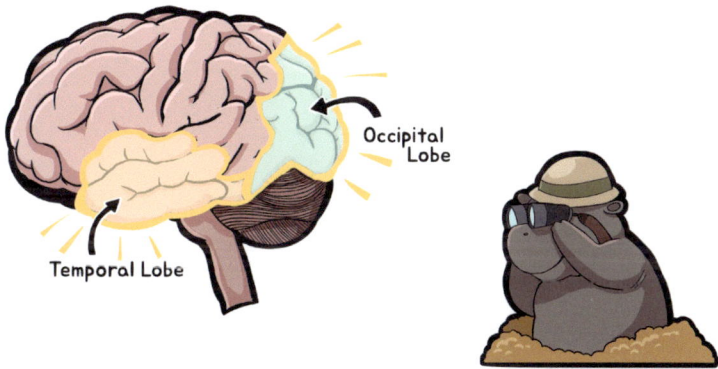

Occipital Lobe

Temporal Lobe

The Cerebellum: Small but Mighty!

by Wayan

The **cerebellum** ('seh-ruh-beh-luhm') is part of the hind brain. Though small, it is packed with brain cells – neurons – and therefore is **especially** wrinkly. Remember, we mentioned earlier that the wrinkles of the brain increase surface area, packing in the neurons which allows for shorter axons and greater efficiency.[25]) It does this especially in the cerebellum.

Wayan

Scientists are discovering many interesting things about the cerebellum. What is especially notable to me is its role in balance. In fact, the cerebellum functions as a regulator of balance control and bodily movements.

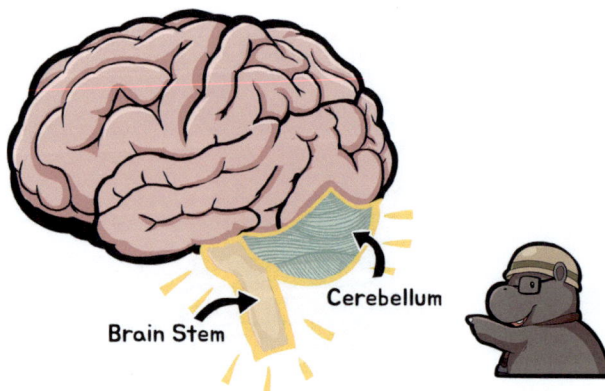

Brain Stem

Cerebellum

When I stand on one leg or land from a leap across the stage, my cerebellum comes into play. It is responsible not only for the posture, accuracy and balance of movements, but also for the fluidity and coordination of those movements.[26]

You can imagine then, that as a dancer, this part of my brain is highly important! The cerebellum also comes into play in athletics and **ALL** movements, including speech. Researchers have also found that language, emotion and memory are related functions here too.

The Amygdala: Learning is Emotional Stuff

by Breda

Learning is emotional stuff and don't let anyone tell you differently! The **amygdala** ('uh-mig-duh-la') is associated with emotions and thus is a good place for us to pause on this whistle stop brain tour! The happy, sad, good and bad can influence whether you learn or don't learn.

Breda

How we feel – comfortable in the classroom or not, good about ourselves or not – are all highly wrapped up in the amygdala within the **limbic system**.[27]

Amygdala

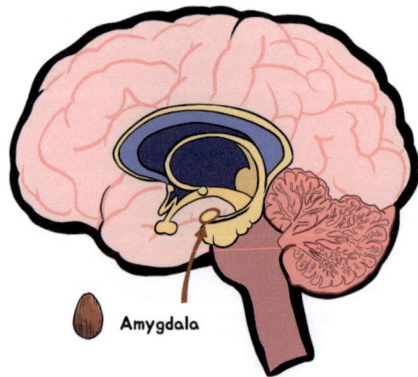

Tucked deep inside the brain, the limbic system is part of the brain's centre, not only for emotions, but also for behaviour and memory. Specifically, the amygdala can be triggered to send signals about what we are feeling or experiencing – whether we are frightened and ready to flee or remain calm and comfortable. The amygdala may be small and almond-shaped (hence its name) but, make no mistake, it is immensely important!

Remember when some of us students felt stressed, frustrated, and initially unsupported back at Grimly Grammar? The amygdala region of our brains was processing these emotions and sending signals to our endocrine ('en-do-krin') system that sends out hormones. When cortisol ('cor-te-sol'), a stress hormone, is released it can block learning.[28]

In contrast, remember how Dr. Calcoolya helped students like me feel validated and empowered with effective learning strategies? Positive learning experiences with encouragement influence the release of oxytocin ('ox-ee-toe-sin') and dopamine ('doe-peh-mean'). Oxytocin is a hormone released when a sense of warmth and trust are felt. Dopamine is released when pleasure is experienced – which includes positive, meaningful and fun learning experiences![29]

There is **a lot** to know about the brain and while, we can't cover **everything** on this safari (next time, right?!) we would be remiss if we did not mention the **hippocampus** … StoddART is a hippo after all! But truth be told, the hippocampus actually has nothing to do with a hippo! The word hippocampus means 'sea horse' because it resembles the small marine animal in shape.

What does it do? The hippocampus plays an important role in memory by consolidating information from short-term memory into long-term memory.[30] (Ultimately, the goal of learning is to remember information that has been processed to make meaning out of it after all!)

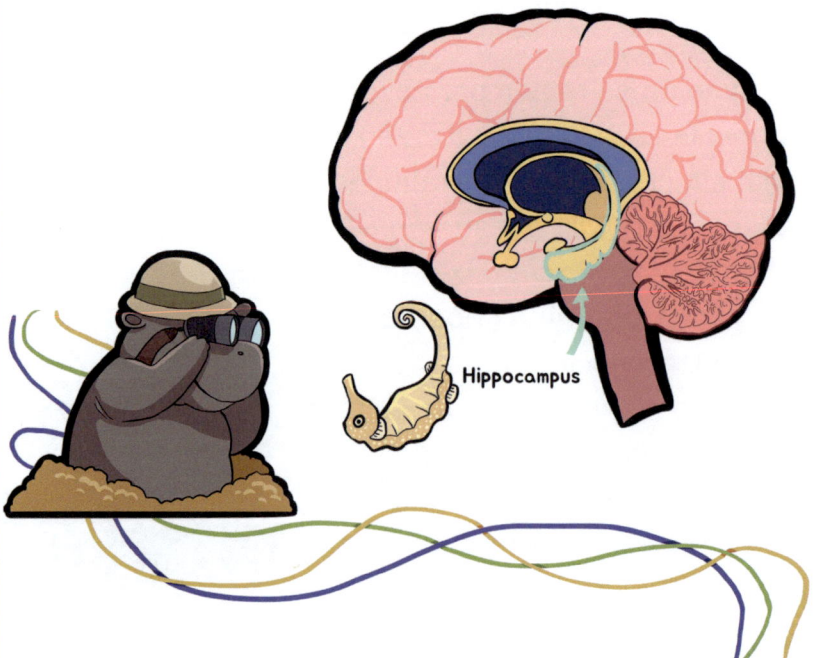

Hippocampus

Thoughts on Working Memory

by Mzumbay

Working memory is an executive skill that requires the brain to hold, use, store and retrieve information while performing a task. This means that information in the short term is manipulated to execute the job at hand, be it solving an equation or decoding a new word. In turn, working memory helps the brain

Mzumbay

organise new information for long-term memory storage for later retrieval. Executive Functioning expert, Tera Sumpter, likens working memory to a juggler juggling several jobs simultaneously.[31]

Scientists are actively learning more about working memory. They know that the stress hormone, cortisol, impairs working memory (and executive functioning in general).[32] Remember when Molly and Mark were put on the spot? This caused them to experience stress so that even if they did know the right answer, it could be hard or even impossible for them to figure it out!

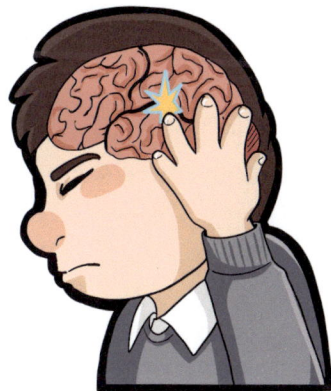

This is why it really pays to have a warm, welcoming school culture, where learning profiles of all kinds are honoured! Some learning experts, like Martha Sweeney, call this **safety of spirit**. This means that school administrators, teachers and fellow students have a common regard for the spirit and well-being of every single member of the school community.

Remember that **all** of these special brain regions we've just covered are parts that **work together**.[33] That said, not everyone comes with the same working memory capacity or development of executive skills. This does not mean that those differences mean a person is not smart – not at all. It does mean that some people do not learn in quite the same way, at the same speed or with the same strengths and needs in terms of their individual brains.

Remember what Mrs Brill said?

Every single person's brain is different. This means that variation – differences – should be expected.[34]

Indeed, with variation you get **brain-based diversity** – **neurodiversity** ('nyur-o-die-ver-si-ty') – of all sorts – and that is a wonderful thing! This also means that different skills come more naturally and easily to some than to others. This goes for all sorts of skills in life, from regulating our emotions, making new friends, to planning ahead for tests, organising a meal, drawing a picture, reading new words or solving a word problem. We all come with different skill sets and everyone – **we mean everyone** – has challenges of some sort. Some challenges people face sometimes regard learning.

Neurodiversity

Common cognitive learning differences

Approximately, one in five ($1/5$) of people in a given population around the world have a cognitive (thinking) learning difference. Learning differences come with a mix of challenges and strengths. There are different degrees to the challenges and they may manifest themselves very differently depending on a person's environment including the schooling and support they receive.[35]

Dyslexia: What it Is and What it Isn't

by Mark, Ian and Lucia

Dyslexia ('dis-lex-ee-eh') is a language-based learning difference that typically causes difficulty with reading, word recognition and spelling. Estimates of dyslexia's prevalence around the world vary depending on the criteria used. (Most studies report that approximately $1/7 - 1/10$ people have dyslexia, while others say $1/5$.) This range may be explained by the fact that there are different types and degrees of dyslexia.[36]

Mark

Regardless, dyslexia is considered the most common and well-understood learning difference.

It is a little ironic, isn't it that a learning difference that has to do with challenges in reading and writing would be hard to say, read, and write?! '**Dys**' means **difficulty** and specifically, difficulty with reading and writing related skills. It is good to remember that it is a brain-based condition causing difficulty in language processing.

Ian

Dys = difficulty

Structured literacy, grounded in the science of reading with speech-to-print, phonetic, sound-based learning has been proven to help people with dyslexia not only read with proficient fluency, but also spell with greater accuracy.[37]

Reading lessons that are based on the 'building blocks of reading,' which are segmenting, blending and phoneme manipulation, actually help, not only dyslexic learners, but all learners, to acquire appropriate reading instruction. Reading is truly complex and involves more than decoding, but also comprehension skills.[38]

Lucia

Like other cognitive learning differences, dyslexia is not a sign of low intelligence. Many people with dyslexia are very bright and demonstrate that there are advantages to this learning profile, such as problem-solving and approaching learning tasks from different angles.[36] Some have said that these other angles of seeing and problem-solving may be more big-picture oriented, visual and hands-on. I think and work in 3-D, as some other people I know do who also have dyslexia. There are many different profiles of dyslexia and not everyone thinks and works this way. In fact, no one person with dyslexia is exactly like the next. Like Mrs Brill said – everyone is unique and thus dyslexic learning profiles are too.

Mark

Dyscalculia: Not Maths Dyslexia

by Wayan and Breda

Dyscalculia ('dis-cal-cyool-ya') is a maths learning difference that affects calculation, computation, and reasoning-related skills. Dyscalculia can be a bit tricky to say and has slight variations in its pronunciations around the world. Note that the condition has the root word '**calc**', referring to calculation.

Wayan

Calling dyscalculia, 'maths dyslexia' (as some people do), is a misnomer that can be a little bit misleading, however. Mathematical processes are quite different from reading and spelling. Like dyslexia, though, dyscalculia has no bearing on a person's intelligence.[39]

Dyscalculia can affect people very differently with different degrees of challenges experienced. Generally, it involves some level of difficulty in understanding mathematical quantities. Additionally, people with this learning difference may have mix-ups when reading, thinking, copying, writing,

Breda

speaking and remembering maths symbols, numbers, maths facts, rules and procedures. Additionally, they may experience struggles with mental figuring, handling money and making conversions.[40]

Some dyscalculic people struggle with telling time, time management and punctuality. People with dyscalculia often have difficulty imagining mathematical abstractions, but as with other cognitive learning differences, profiles vary greatly.[41]

Wayan

Breda, for example, experienced symbol and number mix-ups, yet readily understood how to apply algorithms as a young student. And I wasn't initially able to connect numbers and quantities until taught in more multi-modal ways. Yet, for both of us, using experiential learning, finger-counting, drawing, number lines, ten frames, abacuses and other manipulatives – combined with appropriate and individualised instruction – helped us improve in our abilities!

One key to my success, was teachers replacing passive learning methods with experiential learning through building, modelling and drawing.

Breda

Mathematics Education expert, Dr Jo Boaler, is a big proponent of using fingers and drawings, by the way. She cites that it gives a better feeling for maths with deeper understanding.[42]

It's also worth noting that many students with dyslexia also struggle with dyscalculia as an additional learning difference, called **Understood Dyscalculia**.[43]

Understood Dyscalculia is common, yet unfortunately not as well understood, talked about or celebrated as dyslexia. Nevertheless, we too have great potential and can improve when we are asked to identify, define, illustrate and demonstrate key elements and procedures that play off of our existing strengths![44]

Dysgraphia: More Than Just Handwriting

by George

Dysgraphia ('dis-graf-i-uh') is often associated with awkward pencil grip and handwriting. While this was true for me as a young child, this is not actually the definition of dysgraphia as a learning difference. Dysgraphia is a learning difference rooted in a difficulty with transcription.[45]

George

This means that it impacts skills like handwriting, as well as spacing information on a page, typing and sometimes spelling.[46]

Writing by hand is often labored, slow and illegible for those with dysgraphia, but not always. Indeed, dysgraphia can pose challenges with sizing and spacing of words on a page, as well as written expression overall.

Many dysgraphic learners benefit from occupational therapy (OT) for developing fine motor skills, as well as typing, drawing answers to questions and other reasonable adjustments.[47]

While typing on a computer can be a great accommodation, it is important to have interventions that match an individual learner's particular needs.

Note too, dysgraphia is sometimes lumped right in with dyslexia as one and the same learning difference. Many people with dyslexia have dysgraphia, but dysgraphia is not necessarily dyslexia. Maybe the names and labels aren't important but identifying the root of the problem is. The main challenge dysgraphia poses is one of transcription rather than the decoding and processing of words themselves.

Dyspraxia Takes Many Forms

by Lucia, Molly and Ian

Dyspraxia ('dis-prax-i-uh') is also called Developmental Coordinator Disorder (DCD). It is a learning difference related to **praxis**, meaning action or motor planning. It can involve sensory integration, memory, judgment, processing of information and other cognitive skills.[48]

As you might recall, **dys** means difficulty and **praxis** refers to control of movement. For some people, dyspraxia translates as reduced voluntary control of a singular kind of movement, while for others it might be the sequence or integration of numerous movements.[49]

There are three of us discussing dyspraxia just to show you how variable this condition is!

Multi-step directions are really challenging for me. At first people thought it stemmed from an attentional issue (and plenty of people with dyspraxia do have ADHD).[50] In my case though, it is very hard to integrate information and execute certain physical tasks.

Lucia

As a result, my desk was always messy and often my own appearance was too. Additionally, I found things like learning to ride a bicycle difficult as a small child. Using a balance bike helped. Then with academic tasks, I learned that writing lists, making sequence maps and breaking information down really helped me make things work together as one. I have been an excellent student and successful entrepreneur over my career. Nevertheless, I still need reminding of multi-step directions and my desk is often messy. As for self-care, such as my clothes etc, I've also learned to keep my wardrobe simple.

Many people with dyspraxia experience visual-spatial difficulties and orientation, like remembering their left from their right. This meant that reversing the dance steps in ballet was really tough as a youngster and learning to drive a bit of a process as an adult. Also, when I arrived at Freshton,

Molly

I'd get easily turned around and mixed up. Where was I? Which hallway took me to the dorm versus the activity centre? But with help, whether following ballet steps, or knowing how to get around on campus, having someone patiently talk directions through while showing me the steps, made a huge difference. For example, I am now a great driver!

A key to any challenge in life is to give yourself the due process you need. I know I need a little extra time to visualise steps to help orient myself, so I simply allow for this.[51] I also know how to have a sense of humour about it too. You see, at the root of my issues is the simple fact that I do not have a naturally good sense of direction. I mix up my left from my right. While I used to get terribly flustered and anxious, I now own it! I just hold up my hands and remember that the one that makes the **L** is my **LEFT** hand and the one that doesn't is my right. It's good to learn little things like this that can help along the way in life.

I have excellent eye-hand coordination and am a good athlete, so dyspraxia does not affect me in the same way. As a young child, however, I found pronouncing certain long vowels very difficult. I couldn't pronounce long words or sounds that took more motor coordination than those in simpler sounding words. On top of it, I have dyslexia, so language and literacy issues have been really challenging for me. The key to my success was speech and language therapy for my dyspraxia speech issues. Lip rounding, blowing bubbles, and other methods that targeted my specific needs really helped me. And now? Listen to me! You'd never even know I struggled in this way! Then, for my dyslexia, it was using speech-to-print methods to build decoding skills. Like the other cognitive learning differences, dyscalculia and dysgraphia, dyspraxia has some overlaps with dyslexia.[52]

Ian

Moreover, many people with dyslexia have dyspraxia. Yet these cognitive learning differences are not all one and the same. Getting the right identification is really key so that the right interventions can be put in place.

ADHD: Attention Deficit Hyperactivity Disorder

by Chris and Mzumbay

ADHD (Attention Deficit Hyperactivity Disorder) is categorised as a behaviour difference. It is sometimes lumped in as a learning difference, as it can impact learning. Regardless of classification, attentional issues are common and often connected to students with dyslexia, dyscalculia, dysgraphia and dyspraxia.[53]

Chris

ADHD manifests very differently depending on the learner and in many cases isn't so much an attention deficit, but a condition of hyper-focus. This means a person focuses on the things that interest them and they may forget or disregard tasks and information less desirable to engage in or find less interesting.[54]

Mzumbay

Like other neurodiverse profiles, people with ADHD are often found to be especially creative problem-solvers. Just like the colours in George's paintings, ADHD learners often burst with energy and ideas.[55]

We are ALL More Than One Thing

by Mark, George and Breda

Quite often people with neurodiverse profiles have more than one learning difference, such as dyslexia and dysgraphia, for example. As well as having a learning difference, they may also have a behavioural one. We talked about ADHD – something many people with dyslexia have. There is also Asperger's – a common difference in which a person may struggle with cues in social communication.

Mark

There are many forms of neurodiversity and this is a good reminder that regardless of learning or behaviour profile, **people are more than one thing**. Hence, they may **identify** themselves as more than one thing too. A person might be a scientist **and** mathematics teacher, like Dr Calcoolya. They might be a painter **and** therapist like I am, or a sculptor and dyslexia ambassador like Mark is. They may be a musician **and** an athlete **and** potentially many things.

George

The fact is, people are multi-dimensional and complex – because brains are complex, remember!? And people come with an incredible mix of identities, strengths, interests and challenges in life. That mix is unique to each person and it is worth exploring!

Breda

When it comes to learning, it's worth identifying your own personal brain power: your strengths in all sorts of arenas in life – in school, outside of school, on a sports field, art studio, at camp, wherever. It is also worth identifying your challenges – your need areas.

Spend some time learning about strategies that might help you improve, ones you know of already and ones you don't. Consider learning about new ones. So, give it a go: What are your strengths? What are areas in which you could improve – at school or some other capacity?

Brain Plasticity and a Growth Mindset

Brain plasticity? Huh?! We started this resource section saying that our brains are made of neurons – cells – biological tissue and now we're ending by telling you it's plastic? How can that be? Except that we don't mean plastic material that comes from petroleum. Instead we mean that the brain is flexible – malleable, 'shapeable'. This means the brain is something like a rubber band in a way and also a bit like a plant in another.[56]

It means that those excitable neurons can ignite other excitable neurons, connect and 'grow' more synaptic networks … and those networks can build to be knowledge and skills and all that makes you, **YOU**! Whoever you are and however you learn with grit, determination and appropriate strategies and methods, the brain can be trained.

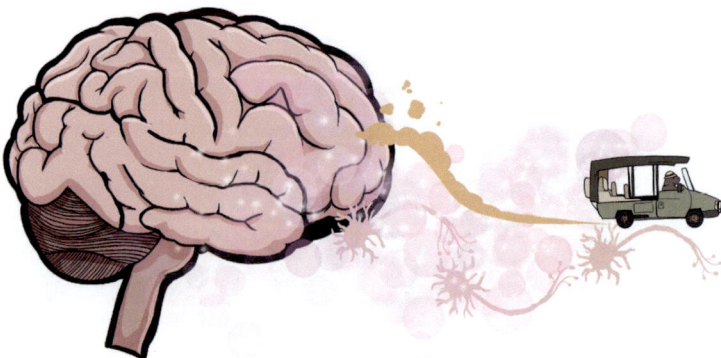

Weak spots can be strengthened and challenges worked upon. And this is not just for kids to note, but adults too. Our brains can change.

It is powerful to consider, therefore, that the brain literally changes from **every** single experience a person has.[57] (This is why positive learning experiences are **so** important and impactful!) It also means that the more we learn, the more we can keep on learning.

Neuroscientist, Dr Eagleman, reminds us: 'Your brain is a relentless shape-shifter, constantly rewriting its own circuitry … because your neural networks continue to change your whole life, your identity is a moving target; it never reaches an endpoint.'[58]

No endpoint! What a powerful notion. That means that learning and growing have endless potential.

(No endpoint also sounds like a circle.) And that brings us back to our initial conversation circling around a table.

A special table and a conversation that marks positive change through a growth – learning safari – mindset!

About the Authors

Mark Stoddart

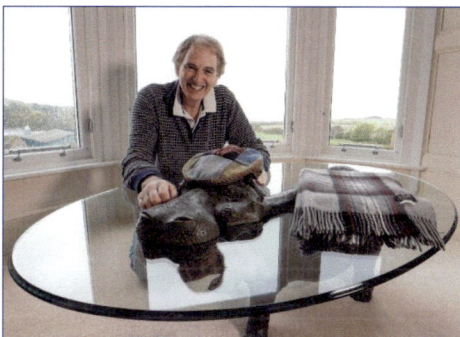

This book is inspired by the life and artwork of Mark Stoddart, whose life really has been safari-like. Struggling with dyslexia and related learning differences, he never thought his life would amount to anything. Everything changed once Mark became equipped with the tools and experiences that released his potential and built his confidence. In addition to being a sculptor, specialising in bronze works, Mark is global ambassador for non-profit charities, like Dyslexia Scotland, Bali Dyslexia and Dyslexia Kenya. He is a big supporter of neurodiverse schools, education and the arts. Mark's bronze sculptures and furniture pieces have become collectables throughout the world. His own success in art stems from his dyslexic thinking, manifested through the creative process and nourished by teachers and other encouraging people in his life. Mark sculpts and helps support schools and young artists on their own learning safaris. Learn more about Mark, his bronze works, neurodiverse schools, and many projects.
https://www.markstoddart.com/

Photo courtesy: Matthew (Matt) Watson Stoddart

Photo courtesy: personal

Photo courtesy: Katrin McElderry

Katrin McElderry

Katrin 'Kate' McElderry is a program director for dyslexia outreach programs and a learning specialist for language and literacy skills. She works at The Odyssey School, a unique evidence-based school in Baltimore County, Maryland for students with dyslexia and other language-based learning differences. Kate is trained in the science of reading and is a seasoned teacher who has taught internationally in a variety of settings. Kate has an intrinsic understanding of the learning safari that neurodiversity can bring

Photo courtesy: Ivana Lalicki

– wild and also wonderful, by virtue of having a form of dyscalculia herself. As with many neurodiverse learners, the arts—visual and dance – were key in learning and developing confidence. Kate believes strongly in neuroscience guiding best practices in teaching and also the power of infusing the arts – as expression, but also as a mechanism for learning. She also believes that reading, sharing and discussing stories can be an empowering journey.

About the Illustrators

Rachel Cush

Rachel Cush is a comic creator and illustrator based in the Scottish Highlands. She is responsible for the majority of drawings in this book, creating original sketches for characters like Mark, Breda, George, Kallie (the dog), Ian, Mr Gruel, Mrs Thwart, Mr Redwell, Mr O'Toole, Dr Calcoolya and other Freshton students. After finishing a degree in Zoology, she worked as an ecologist and artist before pursuing art full time. Rachel loves everything animals and nature and has a keen interest in mythology, spooky stories and folktales. Rachel aims to help more people become interested in science and nature through storytelling and art.

Rossie Stone

Rossie Stone runs Dekko Comics and is a graduate of Duncan of Jordanstone College of Art and Design at the University of Dundee in Scotland. Rossie is responsible for several illustrations for this book including Mr Obliviay, Mrs Brill and the 'A-ha moment' when Mark sees the hippo. Rossie has created the illustrations in many educational books including *Mission Dyslexia*, and actively partakes in dyslexia awareness. He is also, like Mark, a Dyslexia Scotland Ambassador.

Learning Resource/ Brain-based Information Editors

Fumiko Hoeft, MD PhD is a neuroscientist, researcher, professor and internationally known speaker on Literacy acquisition, Dyslexia as well as other Neuroeducational topics. Dr Hoeft was faculty at Stanford University and University of California, San Francisco (UCSF), and is currently the lab director of the Laboratory for Learning Engineering and Neural Systems (brainLENS), a collaboration between researchers at the University of Connecticut (UConn) and UCSF and directs the Brain Imaging Research Center at UConn.

Nirbhay N. Yadav, PhD is an internationally recognised neuroscientist. Dr Yadav recieved his PhD from the University of Western Sydney, Australia and completed a post-doctoral fellowship in Radiology at the Johns Hopkins University School of Medicine. Dr Yadav's laboratory, based at Johns Hopkins and the Kennedy Krieger Institute, is focused on developing advanced neuroimaging methods and applying these techniques to address clinical needs.

Wee Debrief: Discussion Questions and Reflection

1. How do mistakes help us learn?

2. Did you know that there are many ways people are smart and being good at reading and mathematical sums is only one of them? Discuss different ways people are smart.

3. Consider the motto at Grimly Grammar. It states that learning is simple and the goal is to get the right answer. How or why might this motto send the wrong message to the students and teaching staff?

4. The word '**grim**' can mean depressing, terrible, and uninviting. How is Grimly Grammar the very essence of the word 'grim'? Write and/or draw examples.

5. How are the teachers at Grimly Grammar something like their names?
   - ❖ Mr Obliviay
   - ❖ Mrs Thwart
   - ❖ Mr Gruel

6. One of the chapters is called, 'School Fails Mark,' (not Mark Fails School). How does the school fail Mark and some of the other students?

7. Whoever we are and however we learn, everyone benefits from being supported and understood! Through a drawing or list, reflect on what would show support and understanding for you.

8. How does the garden become like an outdoor classroom for learning for Mark? What discoveries does he make? What does he hope his new teachers will be like in the future?

9. The methods taught and materials used at Freshton are very different from what students like Mark, George and Breda experienced before. Compare and contrast the two schools: Grimly Grammar and Freshton College. (Consider revisiting the mottos.)

10. How does Mrs Brill liken learning to a safari?

11. What does Mr Redwell say about language and literacy? Can you recall the four parts in the L + L (Language and Literacy) chart?

12. Discuss Breda's struggles briefly. What strategies help her?

13. George gives Mark advice when he feels overwhelmed. What is it?

14. How are the teachers at Freshton something like their names?
  ❖   Mrs Brill
  ❖   Mr Redwell
  ❖   Dr Calcoolya
  ❖   Mr O'Toole

15. Why did Mr O'Toole give Mark the key to the art studio? What discoveries does Mark make while in the studio?

16. What were some of the bumps in the road that Mark experienced as an adult? What bumps in the road – challenges – have you faced in your life?

17. Describe the '**a-ha** moment' Mark had during his safari. How does it relate to Mrs Brill's idea of a learning safari?

18. What specifically helped to launch Mark's career? Describe some of the sculptures Mark has made.

19. There are a number of analogies – comparisons – made in this book. Learning is compared to a garden and also a safari. When Mark makes his bronze sculptures, he also sees bronze-making much like learning too. Briefly explain why.

20. What are ways you can embrace process (over always being 'right') and a growth mindset in your life?

21. What is the brain sometimes compared to? What are some parts of the brain and what do they do?

22. Students at Freshton reflect different learning profiles. Can you describe them?

23. What is neurodiversity?

24. How are you more than one thing? What helps you learn and be your best?

25. Consider the title of the book: **Making a Mark! Discovering the Power of Neurodiversity on a Learning Safari**. How does 'making a mark' have several meanings?

Work Cited/ Notes

Note to Reader:
Footnotes are a synthesis of information from multiple sources. They are compiled in order of use.

1. Gamwell, Peter and Daley, Jane (2017) *The Wonder Wall: Leading Creative Schools and Organizations in an Age of Complexity*. Thousand Oaks, CA: Corwin

2. Schneps, Matthew (2022), in: DelGaudio, Rob, Giuliano, Rocco and DelGaudio Cecilia (producers) *Blame It On Gutenberg*. Westport, MA: Black Pearl Productions, Inc

3. Wasowicz, Jan (2022), in: DelGaudio, Rob, Giuliano, Rocco and DelGaudio Cecilia (producers) *Blame It On Gutenberg*. Westport, MA: Black Pearl Productions, Inc

    Wasowizc, Jan (30 October 2019) 'The Role of Speech to Print Instruction in Developing Proficiency in Reading and Writing', We All Learn, Stevenson University, Owings Mills, MD (Lecture)

4. Mandela, Nelson (18 May 2002) 90th Birthday Celebration of Walter Sisulu, Walter Sisulu Hall, Randburg, Johannesburg, South Africa. © 2010 by Nelson R. Mandela and The Nelson Mandela Foundation

5. Hoeft, Fumiko (26 February 2021) 'Brain Basics & The Science of Optimism', Ask a Brain Scientist, Haskins Global Literacy Hub for The Odyssey School (Online workshop)

    Hoeft, Fumiko (22 June 2021) 'Brain Workshop for Youth: Learning about the Brain, Dyslexia & More!', Ask a Brain Scientist, Haskins Global Literacy Hub for Flourish Education International Group (Online workshop)

    Duranovic, M., Dedeic, M. and Gavrić, M. (2015) 'Dyslexia and visual-spatial talents', *Current Psychology* 34, pp. 207–222. Available at: https://doi.org/10.1007/s12144-014-9252-3

https://dyslexiaida.org/why-study-dynamic-visual-spatial-thinking-in-dyslexia-qa-with-jeffrey-gilger/

Gilger, J., Talavage, T. & Olulade, O. (2013) 'An fMRI study of nonverbally gifted reading disabled adults: has deficit compensation effected gifted potential?', *Frontiers in Human Neuroscience*, 7, pp. 1-12. Available at: https://doi.org/10.3389/fnhum.2013.00507

Gilger, J. W. & Olulade, O. A. (2013) 'What happened to the "superior abilities" in adults with dyslexia and high IQs? A behavioral and neurological illustration', *Roeper Review*, 35(4), pp. 241-253. Available at: DOI: 10.1080/02783193.2013.825365

https://www.dyslexia.com/about-dyslexia/dyslexic-talents/the-visual-spatial-learner

6. Hoeft, Fumiko (22 June 2021) 'Brain Workshop for Youth: Learning about the Brain, Dyslexia & More!', Ask a Brain Scientist, Haskins Global Literacy Hub for Flourish Education International Group (Online workshop)

    Saltz, Gail (2018) *The Power of Different: The Link Between Disorder and Genius*. New York, NY: Flatiron Books

    Honos-Webb, Lara (2010) *The Gift of ADHD: How to Transform Your Child's Problems into Strengths*. Oakland, CA: New Harbinger Publications

7. Gardner, Howard (2011) *Frames of Mind: The Theory of Multiple Intelligences*. New York, NY: Basic Books

    Saltz, Gail (2018) *The Power of Different: The Link Between Disorder and Genius.* New York, NY: Flatiron Books

8. Saltz, Gail (2018) *The Power of Different: The Link Between Disorder and Genius.* New York, NY: Flatiron Books

9. Yadav, Nirbhay (Pers. comm.)

    https://www.ninds.nih.gov/health-information/public-education/brain-basics/brain-basics-know-your-brain

10-11. Hoeft, Fumiko (26 February 2021) 'Brain 101 For Kids: What Does the Brain Do & How Do We Study It?', Ask a Brain Scientist, Haskins Global Literacy Hub for The Odyssey School (Online workshop)

https://www.ninds.nih.gov/health-information/public-education/brain-basics/brain-basics-know-your-brain

12. https://www.ninds.nih.gov/health-information/public-education/brain-basics/brain-basics-know-your-brain

13. https://www.ninds.nih.gov/health-information/public-education/brain-basics/brain-basics-life-and-death-neuron

Yadav, Nirbhay (Pers. comm.)

Hoeft, Fumiko (Pers. comm.)

Khan Academy 'The neuron and nervous system', Course: Biology Library, Unit 33, Lesson 2. Available at: https://www.khanacademy.org/science/biology/human-biology/neuron-nervous-system/a/the-synapse#:~:text=Most%20synapses%20are%20chemical%3B%20these%20synapses%20communicate%20using,potential%20triggers%20the%20presynaptic%20neuron%20to%20release%20neurotransmitters

14. Yadav, Nirbhay (Pers. comm.)

Hoeft, Fumiko (Pers. comm.)

Krupic, Julija (217) 'Wire together, fire apart', Science, 357 (6355), pp. 974-975. Available at: https://www.science.org/doi/abs/10.1126/science.aao4159#:~:text=This%20principle%20is%20known%20as,fire%20together%E2%80%9D%20(2)

Eagleman, David (2021) Livewired: The Inside Story of the Ever-Changing Brain. New York, NY: Vintage

15. Carroway, Kimberly (23 August 2022) 'Training: Practical Teaching and Learning Strategies', Applying Brain Research to Classroom Instruction, The Odyssey School, Lutherville, MD (Lecture)

Yadav, Nirbhay (Pers. comm.)

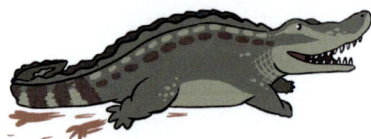

16.   Carroway, Kimberly (23 August 2022) 'Training: Practical Teaching and Learning Strategies', Applying Brain Research to Classroom Instruction, The Odyssey School, Lutherville, MD (Lecture)

17.   Yadav, Nirbhay (Pers. comm.)

Hoeft, Fumiko (Pers. comm.)

Krupic, Julija (217) 'Wire together, fire apart', *Science*, 357 (6355), pp. 974-975. Available at: https://www.science.org/doi/abs/10.1126/science.aao4159#:~:text=This%20principle%20is%20known%20as,fire%20together%E2%80%9D%20(2)

Alcami, Pepe and Pereda, Alberto E (2019) 'Beyond Plasticity; the dynamic impact of electrical synapses on neural circuits' *Nature Reviews. Neuroscience,* 20 (5), pp. 253-271. Available at: https://www.nature.com/articles/s41583-019-0133-5

Pereda, Alberto E (2014) 'Electrical synapses and their functional interactions with chemical synapses', *Nature Reviews Neuroscience,* 15(4), pp. 250.263. Available at: https://www.ncbi.nlm.nih.gov/pmc/articles/PMC4091911/

18.   https://www.ninds.nih.gov/health-information/public-education/brain-basics/brain-basics-know-your-brain

Carroway, Kimberly (23 August 2022) 'Training: Practical Teaching and Learning Strategies', Applying Brain Research to Classroom Instruction, The Odyssey School, Lutherville, MD (Lecture)

19.   https://www.ninds.nih.gov/health-information/public-education/brain-basics/brain-basics-know-your-brain

Sumpter, Tera (11 November 2022) 'Executive Functioning: More Than Just Attention', The Odyssey School, Lutherville, MD (Lecture)

Sumer, Tera (2021) *The Seeds of Learning: A Cognitive Processing Model for Speech, Language, Literacy, and Executive Functioning.* Lakewood, OH: ELH Publishing, LLC

Carroway, Kimberly (23 August 2022) 'Training: Practical Teaching and Learning Strategies', Applying Brain Research to Classroom Instruction, The Odyssey School, Lutherville, MD (Lecture)

20-22. https://www.ninds.nih.gov/health-information/public-education/brain-basics/brain-basics-know-your-brain

23.   https://en.wikipedia.org/wiki/Parietal_lobe

Zaehle, Tino et al. (2007) 'The neural basis of the egocentric and allocentric spatial frame of reference', *Brain Research*, 1137(1), pp.92-103. Available at: https://pubmed.ncbi.nlm.nih.gov/17258693/

Hoeft, Fumiko (Pers. comm.)

https://www.ninds.nih.gov/health-information/public-education/brain-basics/brain-basics-know-your-brain

24-25. Yadav, Nirbhay (Pers. comm.)

Carroway, Kimberly (23 August 2022) 'Training: Practical Teaching and Learning Strategies', Applying Brain Research to Classroom Instruction, The Odyssey School, Lutherville, MD (Lecture)

https://www.ninds.nih.gov/health-information/public-education/brain-basics/brain-basics-know-your-brain

26.   https://www.ninds.nih.gov/health-information/public-education/brain-basics/brain-basics-know-your-brain

27.   Hoeft, Fumiko (26 February 2021) 'Brain 101 For Kids; What Does the Brain Do & How Do We Study It?', Ask a Brain Scientist, Haskins Global Literacy Hub for The Odyssey School (Online workshop)

Jimsheleishvili, Sopiko and Dididze, Marine (24 July 2023) 'Neuroanatomy, cerebellum'. Available at: https://www.ncbi.nlm.nih.gov/books/NBK538167/

Cherry, Kendra (12 May 2023) 'The location and function of the cerebellum in the brain'. Available at: https://www.verywellmind.com/what-is-the-cerebellum-2794964#toc-what-are-the-functions-of-the-cerebellum

28. Carroway, Kimberly (23 August 2022) 'Training: Practical Teaching and Learning Strategies', Applying Brain Research to Classroom Instruction, The Odyssey School, Lutherville, MD (Lecture)

Hoeft, Fumiko (26 February 2021) 'Brain 101 For Kids: What Does the Brain Do & How Do We Study It?', Ask a Brain Scientist, Haskins Global Literacy Hub for The Odyssey School (Online workshop)

29. Guy-Evans, Olivia (19 September 2023) 'What is the limbic system? Definition, parts, and functions', *Simply Psychology*. Available at: https://www.simplypsychology.org/limbic-system.html

Hoeft, Fumiko (22 June 2021) 'Brain Workshop for Youth: Learning about the Brain, Dyslexia & More!', Ask a Brain Scientist, Haskins Global Literacy Hub for Flourish Education International Group (Online workshop)

Carroway, Kimberly (23 August 2022) 'Training: Practical Teaching and Learning Strategies', Applying Brain Research to Classroom Instruction, The Odyssey School, Lutherville, MD (Lecture)

Wied, D (1976) 'Hormonal influences on motivation, learning, and memory processes', *Hospital Practice*, 11(1), pp.123-31. Available at: DOI: 10.1080/21548331.1976.11706486

Sumpter, Tera (11 November 2022) 'Executive Functioning: More Than Just Attention', The Odyssey School, Lutherville, MD (Lecture)

30. Carroway, Kimberly (23 August 2022) 'Training: Practical Teaching and Learning Strategies', Applying Brain Research to Classroom Instruction, The Odyssey School, Lutherville, MD (Lecture)

Hoeft, Fumiko (26 February 2021) 'Brain 101 For Kids: What Does the Brain Do & How Do We Study It?', Ask a Brain Scientist, Haskins Global Literacy Hub for The Odyssey School (Online workshop)

31. Sumpter, Tera (11 November 2022) 'Executive Functioning; More Than Just Attention', The Odyssey School, Lutherville, MD (Lecture)

    Carroway, Kimberly (23 August 2022) 'Training: Practical Teaching and Learning Strategies', Applying Brain Research to Classroom Instruction, The Odyssey School, Lutherville, MD (Lecture)

32-33. Carroway, Kimberly (23 August 2022) 'Training: Practical Teaching and Learning Strategies', Applying Brain Research to Classroom Instruction, The Odyssey School, Lutherville, MD (Lecture)

    Sumpter, Tera (11 November 2022) 'Executive Functioning; More Than Just Attention', The Odyssey School, Lutherville, MD (Lecture)

34. Saltz, Gail (16 November 2019) 'The Power of Different' Neurodiversity. The Link Between Disorder and Genius, The Odyssey School, Lutherville, MD (Lecture)

35. Hoeft, Fumiko (Pers. comm.)

    dyslexiaida.org

    Baumer, Nicole and Frueh, Julia (23 November 2021) 'What is neurodiversity?' *Harvard Health Publishing*, Harvard Medical School. Available at: https://www.health.harvard.edu/blog/what-is-neurodiversity-202111232645

36. Baumer, Nicole and Frueh, Julia (23 November 2021) 'What is neurodiversity?' *Harvard Health Publishing*, Harvard Medical School. Available at: https://www.health.harvard.edu/blog/what-is-neurodiversity-202111232645

    Hoeft, Fumiko (Pers. comm.)

    dyslexiaida.org

    dyslexiascotland.org.uk

    https://dyslexia.ie/

37. https://learningbydesign.com/

    https://phono-graphix.com/

38.   Wasowizc, Jan (30 October 2019) 'The Role of Speech to Print Instruction in Developing Proficiency in Reading and Writing', We All Learn, Stevenson University, Owings Mills, MD (Lecture)

https://phono-graphix.com/

https://learningbydesign.com/why-spell-links/

https://www.thereadingleague.org/

39.   Sudha, P and Shalini, A (April 2014) 'Dyscalculia: A specific learning disability among children', *Journal of Scientific and Technical Information Processing,* 2(4), pp.912-918. Available at: https://www.researchgate.net/publication/262188807_Dyscalculia_A_Specific_Learning_Disability_Among_Children

Lyons I, Beilock SL. (31 October 2012) 'When math hurts: Math anxiety predicts pain network anticipation of doing math', *PLOS One*, 7(10): e48076. Available at: DOI: 10.1371/journal.pone.0048076

Price GR and Ansari D. (2013) 'Dyscalculia: characteristics, causes and treatments', *Numeracy*, 6(1). Available at: DOI: http://dx.doi.org/10.5038/1936-4660.6.1.2

https://www.understood.org/en/articles/what-is-dyscalculia

40.   https://www.understood.org/en/articles/what-is-dyscalculia

https://www.youtube.com/watch?v=IezO567SKNM

Sudha, P and Shalini, A (April 2014) 'Dyscalculia: A specific learning disability among children', *Journal of Scientific and Technical Information Processing,* 2(4), pp.912-918. Available at: https://www.researchgate.net/publication/262188807_Dyscalculia_A_Specific_Learning_Disability_Among_Children

Lyons I, Beilock SL. (31 October 2012) 'When math hurts: Math anxiety predicts pain network anticipation of doing math', *PLOS One*, 7(10): e48076. Available at: DOI: 10.1371/journal.pone.0048076

Price GR and Ansari D. (2013) 'Dyscalculia: characteristics, causes and treatments', *Numeracy*, 6(1). Available at: DOI: http://dx.doi.org/10.5038/1936-4660.6.1.2

www.dyscalculia.org/home/about

https://simplyhealth.today/14-common-signs-symptoms-of-dyscalculia/?utm_source= %2Bdyscalculia&utm_medium=14CommonSigns& SymptomsofDyscalculia&utm_campaign=adw_us&msclkid=3ae507adb517159f9f5c638c0e7e19f9

41.   https://www.understood.org/en/articles/what-is-dyscalculia

https://www.youtube.com/watch?v=IezO567SKNM

42.   https://www.kqed.org/mindshift/44707/why-kids-should-keep-using-theirs-fingers-to-do-math#:~:text=Stanford%20professor%20Jo%20Boaler%20writes%20in%20The%20Atlantic,research%2C%20be%20akin%20to%20halting%20their%20mathematical%20development

https://ed.stanford.edu/in-the-media/why-kids-should-use-their-fingers-math-class-commentary-jo-boaler

43-44. https://www.understood.org/en/articles/what-is-dyscalculia

https://www.youtube.com/watch?v=IezO567SKNM

45.   Nelson, Holly (11 January 2023) 'Signs that Point to Students Needing OT Evaluation', Dysgraphia & Occupational Therapy, The Odyssey School, Lutherville, MD (Lecture-Training)

https://www.ninds.nih.gov/health-information/disorders/dysgraphia

46-47. Nelson, Holly (11 January 2023) 'Signs that Point to Students Needing OT Evaluation', Dysgraphia & Occupational Therapy., The Odyssey School, Lutherville, MD (Lecture-Training)

48.   https://www.healthline.com/health/dyspraxia

https://en.wikipedia.org/wiki/Developmental_coordination_disorder

Sumpter, Tera (11 November 2022) 'Executive Functioning: More Than Just Attention', The Odyssey School, Lutherville, MD (Lecture)

49. Nelson, Holly (11 January 2023) 'Signs that Point to Students Needing OT Evaluation', Dysgraphia & Occupational Therapy', The Odyssey School, Lutherville, MD (Lecture-Training)

https://www.healthline.com/health/dyspraxia

50. https://www.psychologytoday.com/us/conditions/dyspraxia

https://www.dyspraxiauk.com/

51. Carroway, Kimberly (23 August 2022) 'Training: Practical Teaching and Learning Strategies', Applying Brain Research to Classroom Instruction, The Odyssey School, Lutherville, MD (Lecture)

52. https://www.understood.org/en/articles/understanding-dyspraxia

Nelson, Holly (11 January 2023) 'Signs that Point to Students Needing OT Evaluation', Dysgraphia & Occupational Therapy, The Odyssey School, Lutherville, MD (Lecture-Training)

53. Dawson, Peg (23 March 2019) 'Smart but Scattered: ADHD & Executive Functioning Disorder', Summit School, Edgewater, MD (Lecture-Training)

Carroway, Kimberly (23 August 2022) 'Training: Practical Teaching and Learning Strategies', Applying Brain Research to Classroom Instruction, The Odyssey School, Lutherville, MD (Lecture)

Sumpter, Tera (11 November 2022) 'Executive Functioning: More Than Just Attention', The Odyssey School, Lutherville, MD (Lecture)

54. Dawson, Peg. (23 March 2019) 'Smart but Scattered: ADHD & Executive Functioning Disorder', Summit School, Edgewater, MD (Lecture)

55. Honos-Webb, Lara (2010) *The Gift of ADHD: How to Transform Your Child's Problems into Strengths.* Oakland, CA: New Harbinger Publications

56. Hoeft, Fumiko (26 February 2021) 'Brain 101 For Kids; What Does the Brain Do & How Do We Study It?', Ask a Brain Scientist, Haskins Global Literacy Hub for The Odyssey School (Online workshop)

57. Carroway, Kimberly (23 August 2022) 'Training: Practical Teaching and Learning Strategies' , Applying Brain Research to Classroom Instruction, The Odyssey School, Lutherville, MD (Lecture)

58. Eagleman, David (2017) *The Brain: The Story of You.* New York, NY: Vintage

More Resources

Most parts of the world have non-profit organisations dedicated to helping people with dyslexia and neurodiversity. Here are some links, resources and groups who may be able to help you learn more.

Diversity Celebration Week
https://www.neurodiversityweek.com/

Understood
www.understood.org

Eye to Eye (Neurodiversity)
https://eyetoeyenational.org/

Dyslexia Bytes
https://www.youtube.com/dyslexiabytes
www.dyslexiabytes.org/

Learning Disabilities Association of America
https://ldaamerica.org/about-us/

International Dyslexia Association
https://dyslexiaida.org/

British Dyslexia Association
https://www.bdadyslexia.org.uk/

Dyslexia Scotland
https://dyslexiascotland.org.uk/

Dyslexia Association of Ireland
https://dyslexia.ie/

Dyslexia Kenya
https://www.dyslexiakenya.org/

Bali Dyslexia
https://www.balidyslexiafoundation.org/

Australian Dyslexia Association
https://dyslexiaassociation.org.au/

Dyslexia Association of India
https://dyslexiaindia.org.in/

Dyslexia Association of Singapore
https://www.das.org.sg/

International Federation of Dyslexia and Dyscalculia Associations
https://www.ifdda.org/

Seeds of Learning
https://terasumpter.com/seeds-of-learning

Structured Literacy
https://learningbydesign.com/
https://phono-graphix.com/

Blame It on Gutenberg
https://blameitongutenberg.org

The Wonder Wall: Leading Creative Schools and Organizations in an Age of Complexity, Peter Gamwell and Jane Daly
https://corwin-connect.com/2017/05/whats-wonder-wall/

Acknowledgements

From Mark and Kate

A big shout out and many thanks to Priscilla Hannaford and the team at Brilliant Publications. We thank you for believing in this project and the power of neurodiversity. You are BRILLIANT!

A HUGE thank you to the very talented artists Rachel Cush and Rossie Stone for helping the book come to life with their wonderful illustrations! Rossie, thanks for jumpstarting the process! Rachel, heartfelt thanks for making this massive project happen with a wee babe to look after. We could not have done this without you!

Thank you to our esteemed brain scientists for playing an important role in editing the brain-based resource pages.

Dr Hoeft, we appreciate you meeting with us in the early stages and also inspiring us to infuse brain basics through your Ask A Brain Scientist workshops and other related outreach that empower youth, parents, and educators in the world of education and neurodiversity.

Dr Yadav, thank you so much for reviewing the brain information and suggesting important and relevant facts about current research relating to brain plasticity. Thank you also for making such great suggestions about age-appropriate analogies for kids.

Special thanks to Cathy Magee, CEO of Dyslexia Scotland for her generous time and support. We appreciate the readings, suggestions and encouragement, and the work you do to give dyslexia a voice. Thank you for all you do to support people with dyslexia at all stages of life.

Thank you to Rosie Bissett, for providing feedback and reminding us all that dyslexia and neurodiversity, 'deserve ongoing conversation.' (The book is structured as a big conversation as a result!) Thank you for this and for all you do for Dyslexia

Association of Ireland and European Dyslexia Association.

Thank you Elizabeth Cannon, CCC-SLP for offering your speech-language lens and enthusiastic support.

Many thanks to Phil Burns for helping tease apart content and delivery in the early stages.

Dr Martin Bloomfield, thank you for your generous time, resources, feedback and relentless optimism in the field of neurodiversity.

Thank you, Frewen College, Sussex, UK, for providing inspiration for the book and transforming lives like Mark's through the school's methodology, ethos, kindness, and caring.

Thank you to The Odyssey School, Maryland, USA, for also demonstrating a model school: evidence-based practices, joyful, life-long learning for students and staff alike.

We also wish to express our appreciation to authors, Julie McNeill and Paul McNeill, for their support for this project from its inception and also for the work they do to help children with dyslexia/ neurodiversity.

From Mark

I would like to take a moment to express my heartfelt gratitude to the incredible individuals and institutions that have played pivotal roles in shaping my life and supporting my journey. Their influence has been instrumental during some of the most crucial phases of my development, and I want to acknowledge their contributions with deep appreciation.

First and foremost, I would like to recognise Nel Worth, maiden name de Ruyter de Wildt, who was an inspiring role model and a pillar of support throughout my youth and life. Nel's unwavering belief in me has been a driving force in my life, and I am profoundly grateful for her guidance and encouragement.

144

I would also like to extend my gratitude to the Headmaster and teachers at Brickwall House School, now known as Frewen College, for their dedication and support during my formative years. Their commitment to nurturing young minds has left an indelible mark on my journey.

A special nod of thanks goes to my parents, Matthew and Margaret Stoddart, who made my education at Brickwall House School possible. Their sacrifices and unwavering belief in my potential have been the foundation of my accomplishments.

To my dear friends Tommy Dodds, Ian Irving and Phil Burns, I want to express my sincere appreciation for your friendship, which has been a source of strength and joy in my life. Your unwavering support has been invaluable.

I must also acknowledge Sir Jackie Stewart, whose guidance and inspiration have been a constant source of motivation. Your mentorship has had a profound impact on my path.

In my artistic endeavours, I am deeply grateful to Brian Caster at The Foundry at Powder Hall Bronze for his unwavering support. Your belief in my creative pursuits has been instrumental in my artistic journey.

To Maggi, who tirelessly works behind the scenes to ensure the smooth execution of my numerous projects, I extend my heartfelt thanks. Your dedication is truly appreciated.

Rachael, Karen and the team at Staunton Rook, thank you for your invaluable contributions and hard work. Your efforts have not gone unnoticed.

Ken Masson and Anne Musalia, I am deeply thankful for your assistance, especially with the Kenyan Government, and for your unwavering support in my various projects.

I also want to acknowledge the incredible work of Dr Andrea Carroll, Nancy Munyi, Phyllis Munyi and all others involved in neurodiverse schools and related projects. Together, we are making a profound difference in the lives of young people, and I am honoured to be a part of this impactful journey.

Cathy Magee and her team from Dyslexia Scotland, your mentorship and support in my dyslexia charity endeavours have been truly remarkable. Your dedication is immeasurable, and I am grateful for everything you've done. I am donating all of my royalties for this book to Dyslexia Scotland, to help them continue their excellent work.

At Hamilton and Inches Jewellers in Edinburgh, I would like to express my gratitude to the dedicated team, especially David James Ramsay, Jackie Fowler, Alan Sewell and Frances Desoisa, for their exceptional work and support.

I also extend my thanks to Fiona McDougall at the Scottish Parliament for her invaluable assistance.

Further, I would like to express my gratitude to Geoffrey Matthews at The Chelsea Arts Club and my fellow members for their consistent support and encouragement. Additionally, the Worldwide Rotary Club, I am thankful for the community and the difference we are making together.

My heartfelt acknowledgement would certainly be lacking if I did not shine a spotlight on the exceptional dedication and effort Kate McElderry, my co-author, has brought to this book. From the initial conceptualization to the final touches, Kate's unwavering commitment, depth of knowledge and meticulous attention to detail have been nothing short of exemplary. The synergy between our thoughts and her outstanding craftsmanship has truly elevated the content and narrative of this work. This book is as much a testament to her brilliance and passion as it is to our collaborative journey.

Lastly, I want to say a heartfelt thank you to Sandra, for all her support with my numerous projects.

In conclusion, I am immensely grateful to all these individuals and institutions for their unwavering support, guidance and inspiration. Together, we are shaping a better future and making a positive impact in the lives of young people. Thank you from the bottom of my heart.

From Kate

Deepest gratitude to Mark Stoddart for generously sharing his story and art, and making this collaboration an enriching, enjoyable, and inspiring experience. Heartfelt and deepest thanks to my first and best teacher, my incredible mother. Special appreciation to my late grandparents, who modeled the power of grit and resilience in their own journeys. Heaps of love and appreciation to my wonderfully supportive husband, David Curson, and our children, Seamus, Mary Kells, and Alistair – a constant source of joy and creative inspiration! Hugs and thanks to my creative brother, Kevin, and also to my Aunt Edna for her encouragement and librarian's lens.

A huge thank you to Gen and the Reder Family for so generously opening both home and hearts during my journey. Much love to my in-laws in Britain – thank you for your support and all you do. And to the Irish cohort in Baltimore, Dublin and the West: go raibh maith agat – infinite thanks for your support. To Paul and Olga Ferguson, Caroline and Jimmy McCloy, Ivana Lalicki, Richa Mehta, Ken Saltzberg, Vartika Yadav, and Rachel Fogel, much gratitude for your encouragement over the years.

A special thank you to author, Jack Harte, for generously sharing Forge Corner Writer's Retreat in Sligo, Ireland. While there, he kindly and enthusiastically discussed the initial draft of the book, reminding me of the importance of dialogue by virtue of his own example. Thanks also to author, David Donohue, for sharing writing tips in the early stages.

Thank you David Fink and Eye to Eye for modelling for neurodiverse, by neurodiverse. To the creators of Blame It On Gutenberg, Rob DelGaudio, Rocco Guiliano and Cecilia DelGaudio, a big applause for producing a documentary that explains structured literacy so well, also putting reading in context of human history. Dr Cyndi Burnett and Barney Saltzbeg, hats off for promoting creativity as a valid and important skill in the world of education.

Phyllis Barton and Chris Magarian, much gratitude for early mentoring and hands-on learning. Thank you to my professors and friends from Ripon, Peace Corps, and the Education Department at UMBC for paving the way for exciting learning and teaching opportunities.

Garrison Forest School, The Chewonki Foundation, and The Odyssey School, a standing ovation for being places of academic excellence and personal transformations. (The gift of being part of these communities has lasted a lifetime.)

Much gratitude to Martha Sweeney, and all of my collegues at Odyssey – everyone one of you, upfront and behind the scenes, makes our ship sail! A special nod to Jesse Stiteler, Liz Cannon, and Lisa Waters for being such incredible teacher-collaborators up in the pod with me and also the Odyssey Tutoring Department and Outreach Team for your support. Also, recognising Dr Jan Wasowiscz for excellent training and work in the world of speech-to-print reading and writing methodology – and all others who help in the world of evidence-based teaching.

Last, but not least, a special thank you to my students, past and present, who continue to motivate and inspire me beyond measure.

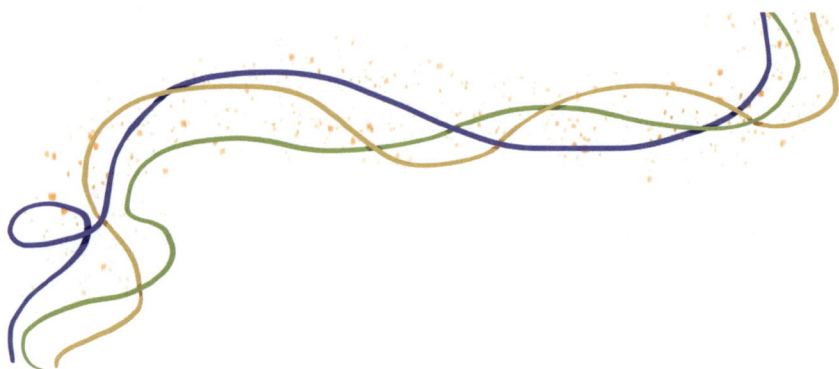

Praise for
Making a Mark! Discovering the Power of Neurodiversity on a Learning Safari

Mark's inspiring life story is set out in an engaging and witty way, which is easy to read and makes us want to know what happens next. There are also serious messages within the story about the significant impact teachers have on young people's lives. The book cleverly combines Mark's dyslexia journey with the learning resources section, which helpfully reinforces the different learning differences experienced by Mark and his classmates. Kate's writing has a gentle sense of humour and a friendly and inclusive approach and the beautiful illustrations aid the readability and accessibility of this must-have book.

Cathy Magee, Scotland

Kate and Mark's book shares Mark's journey with dyslexia with both honesty and hope. The Learning Resources section is packed with interesting facts and insights from young people sharing their experiences of dyslexia, dyscalculia and neurodiversity which is sure to prompt rich discussions and deepen understanding in classrooms and homes worldwide.

Rosie Bissett, Ireland

Making a Mark! Discovering the Power of Neurodiversity on a Learning Safari is a whimsical story inspired by a true character, Mark, the science of reading and learning differences. This book is for learners of ALL ages and profiles, as it teaches us the true challenges that neurodiverse learners face, but at the same time how each of us are different. It highlights the importance of the science of reading, strengths based approaches and resilience. Loved reading it!!! *Dr Fumiko Hoeft, USA*

Katrin McElderry and Mark Stoddart certainly 'hit the mark' with this gem of a book highlighting neurodiversity in story format that both middle school adolescence and adults alike can relate to. It's both fun and funny, while tackling important topics with clarity and sensitivity. Who hasn't had teachers that could be named Mr Obliviay, Mr Thwart, and Mrs Gruel!? Get ready to be thoroughly entertained while learning about neurodiversity, ADHD, and most importantly, safety of spirit.

Elizabeth Cannon, CCC-SLP USA

The book is an inspiration, an exploration, and a celebration. It celebrates the life of a child who struggled; and through his struggles he found a way; and in finding a way, he brought new hope to others. From a difficult start in life, the young protagonist, Mark, showed that children like him could help others make a fresh start. And it's this fresh start that finishes the book, inviting its readers to see that the next stage of the journey is theirs.

Dr Martin Bloomfield, England